SEO Help: 20 Practical Steps to Power your Content Creation, Marketing and Branding in the new AI World of Google Search

SEO Help

20 Practical Steps to Power your Content Creation, Marketing and Branding in the new AI World of Google Search

David Amerland

Online Success Series

ISBN: 1-84481-030-5
ISBN 13: 978-1-84481-030-7

 This edition published 2020

SEO Help: 20 Practical Steps to Power your Content Creation, Marketing and Branding in the new AI World of Google Search.

Published by New Line Books, New York, NY., U.S.A.

This Book can be purchased in electronic format at all major online retailers including Amazon.

SEO Help: 20 Practical Steps to Power your Content Creation, Marketing and Branding in the new AI World of Google Search

David Amerland's involvement with the Web goes back to the days when the number of websites in existence could fit in a printed 80-page directory and SEO consisted of keyword stuffing and pixel-wide hidden text. Since those less enlightened days he has worked with blue-chip multinationals and individual entrepreneur's alike helping them craft SEO and social media marketing strategies that work with their internal cultures and deliver value to their target audience.

He is the author of nine best-selling books including *The Tribe That Discovered Trust* and *Google Semantic Search*. He writes for Forbes and Inc.com and blogs on his own website: DavidAmerland.com. When he is not writing or surfing the Web he spends time giving speeches internationally on how search and social media are changing everything. His latest book is *The Sniper Mind* a deep dive into the world of neuroscience, critical decision making and brain analytics.

Online Success Series

Acknowledgements

No book I write these days is entirely mine. The ideas, suggestions and practices I promote are the result of interactions with the thoughts, case studies, circumstances and practical issues of many others. Some of these are clients of mine with a global presence and, by request, will have to remain anonymous. Others are friends or colleagues who are too numerous to mention. Some have contributed exceptionally with their insights and expertise when engaging with me. Of those I would like to mention in this volume are Teodora Petkova whose book "The Brave New Text: Perspectives on Web Writing" is a vital addition to the ongoing conversation regarding search, language and the semantic web, Dawn Anderson of *Move It Marketing* whose late night shares of research made my late nights later than usual and Bill Slawski to whom any SEO worth his salt owes an incredible debt for his indefatigable analysis of Google patents. Since I last wrote this book Bennie has been added to my personal tribe and he's a time-sink. If this update came out a little later than planned, he is to blame. To all of you who find the time, energy and enthusiasm to take part in my thought experiments and the discussions they spark, "Thank You". You all know who you are and you make a writer's and analyst's life way less isolated than it would otherwise be.

SEO Help: 20 Practical Steps to Power your Content Creation, Marketing and Branding in the new AI World of Google Search

Dedication

The world of business is complex. You all turn up every day and do your thing hoping to get it right. This book is for you all.

Online Success Series

Table of Contents

It's still all about being found!

The very first edition of this book came out in 2010 and a lot has changed in search in that time. SEO has gone from an acronym which constantly needs to be explained to a term which underpins many of the activities of every webmaster and every business.

During this time search itself has also changed. It has become, for a start, the de facto means through which we navigate the web. It has also matured and fragmented. Google still dominates the web as far as search is concerned but search has splintered across video and mobile, social media and apps, to name but just four massive traffic-building channels.

YouTube is the second most popular search engine on the web with over three billion searches a month. Google has managed to become the dominant player in mobile search and search results delivered across mobile devices and is rapidly moving to secure its presence in digital assistants, home assistants and voice search.

As a result, search, these days, is about being found not just in traditional, desktop based searches but also being found on the go, through mobile devices and tablets, being found in apps when those who use them least expect to find you and being found on search, in search queries that still reflect what your business does but for which you may have never thought to optimize your website.

In few other marketing activities does the phrase "the more things change, the more they remain the same" hold as much meaning as it does in search.

In the intervening years since *SEO Help* v1.0 came out to a lot of acclaim search has gone from an activity that entered a business' marketing toolkit as an afterthought to being one that is directly responsible for the success of any business. In plain speak Search *is* Marketing. If your business cannot be found on the web it cannot do business.

It really has become that simple.

This also begs the question on what you need to do. The original *SEO Help* had a simple premise: it offered you 20 search engine optimization steps. It did not explain why you had to take them, nor how they impacted on search engine technology to help your website rise in rankings. I considered theoretical knowledge to be one of those things that are nice to know but not necessary in order to make something work. In the context of the book this is a belief that I still hold. Search however has fragmented to such an extent that I could easily give you 40 – 60 maybe even 100 steps to take, this time round and perhaps not even cover it adequately.

Obviously I haven't done that.

I have still kept this book to 20 steps, though these now are new steps, almost entirely. The approach I have implemented is so good in helping you understand what it is you need to do, that in 2018 "SEO Help" made Book Authority's list of "best SEO Books of all time" - http://bit.ly/2EgNUOZ.

In this edition I have taken into account the fact that technical SEO has receded ever deeper into the website mechanics and non-technical SEO has risen a lot more in importance. Graph-building, ontologies and artificial intelligence have changed search drastically and will continue to do so.

As a result, I have also consciously moved away from the ten questions at the end of each chapter that were the highlight of the earlier editions of this book to ten actionable points you can carry out.

Throughout this book I have factored in Semantic Search as it now plays a key role in the way search evolves across the web. And I have fully taken into account the fact that search now is all about intercept marketing. It's not just about getting your website to rank higher for specific search terms anymore because the idea that you could simply outrank your competitors and get more business this way has, itself, undergone a fundamental change.

Being first on the first page of Google makes less sense than ever because "the first page of Google" has fragmented and mutated to the point that it is virtually different for every person using a search engine, looking for something, through their device.

So, while being "first on the first page of Google" is still important, the idea of 'first' or rather the value of it; has changed almost as radically as the first page of Google itself. What counts today are conversions from online visitors to customers and being found at just the right moment when those looking for your products or services are sufficiently highly motivated to commit to a purchase or similar transactional behavior.

With these two thoughts in mind these 20 Steps to SEO success have, as before, not explained the "why" but they do, always, detail the "what".

Follow them and you will see a couple of things happening: first your website ranking will improve. That's a given. But second, and more important you will increase the targeted visitor numbers to your website. These will be visitors actively looking to find you, who will be finding you through unexpected avenues.

These visitors, the ones who really want to know what your online business does, are also the ones most likely to want to do business with you. It is these you need the most and it is these that this book will help you find.

In the preface to the very first edition of this book I wrote, somewhat naively perhaps, that SEO may go away some time soon. I was not entirely wrong. SEO as an activity that aims to game Google search has, largely gone away. Websites of low quality that appeared on the search results without deserving to be there have also, mostly, gone away. In many ways the SEO mentality of the past is well and truly gone. But SEO defined as search engine optimization that helps your website get indexed better, faster so it can be found more easily is never truly going to go away.

The reason for this lies in the underlying complexities that are found in the intersection where search technology meets website building technology, meets browser technology meets online visitor behavior.

These are complexities that do not concern us here however. What you need to know is that in the brave new world of semantic search and mobile marketing you have a practical 20-step guide that will help your business do more business, find more customers and make more money.

Make it happen.

David Amerland

User Guide

It's ironic that a book that's been written with ease of use in mind should need a user guide on how to use it. *SEO Help* has been written so that each chapter, though part of a progression, is largely autonomous.

As a result you could start from the last chapter and work your way to the front, though personally I would not recommend it. You can dip into any chapter you think will help you right now.

Or you could do the conventional thing and simply start from chapter one and work your way through to chapter twenty.

You must, however, *always* make sure that you go through the Action Checklist at the end of each chapter and perform each task listed there.

Whatever you decide to do, it'll work. This book is practical through and through. Each chapter is a step that gives you an insight in what you have to do in order to get your website to rank higher. It will also help your website be found, have more traffic and more customers. In the process you will also come to understand your business better which will have a welcome, positive impact in the way you brand it and market it.

Step #1

Create a Google Account

 # A Google Account is central to the success of your online identity.

If you are still wondering whether to create a Google Account or not you should have one already!

There is some debate in the SEO industry whether giving access to your privacy to Google is a good thing or not and whether Google still is a "Do not be Evil" company as its motto used to proclaim. The fact that Google quietly removed that motto from its website speaks volumes about the way the company has changed and the web, itself, is evolving.

I have an opinion about that informed by my dealings with many companies and online businesses but in this context it's immaterial. There are two things right now that you need to keep in mind. First that Google's recently updated privacy guidelines are no different to those of Microsoft and Yahoo and they are heck of a lot better than Apple's and Amazon's and second that the moment you get online to work you should give up any serious expectation of privacy.

That doesn't mean that everything you do should be on the web but you should not expect anything you put on the public web to be hidden for long.

If you have not got a Google Account point your browser at: http://accounts.google.com/ and create one.

Make sure you fill it out completely and, incidentally, subscribe for, at the very least: Gmail, Google Analytics, Webmaster Tools, Docs, Google Maps, anything, in short, you find of value amongst Google's services.

There is a good reason for that and it's based on the fact that Google uses all of this to accumulate data about yourself, who you are and what you're doing. It is suitably anonymized so only the patterns of your online behavior are logged in. It all, however, goes to automatically fill in Google's understanding of your online profile and generate the trust Google places in your digital presence.

For the same reason you should be logged into your Google account when carrying out Google searches and when interacting with others on social media networks.

The 'social signature' you generate is very much part of your digital footprint and Google uses it to show you results in search that are relevant to you. More than that however, Google uses the data to assess your importance and influence on the web.

If you are ever going to be successful in the new search reality that has developed, you will need to have an online presence that is capable of acquiring a little 'weight' at least and leveraging some influence, if not your own then that of others. To achieve any of this you need to now establish a visible online identity.

If you are new to all this you will see that upon signing up for a Google Account, Google will most probably require you to also sign into Chrome, as a web browser. Do it! Again, I am not going to debate the right and wrong aspects of this. Right now what you want is to be able to promote your business online and have your site rank high on Google search, in response to relevant search queries. Use Chrome as your browser and, if you can, take advantage of some of the SEO tools that come as extensions to it.

One last word of warning. If you're tempted to create more than one Gmail account thinking that it will help amplify your presence and ability to market, resist it. You may have more than one Gmail address for personal and professional use but the days of creating multiple accounts and online identities to use to artificially boost a website or a promotion are now behind us.

Google can see all this activity even if you have not linked anything in any obvious way. So treat your online identity with the same care and attention that you treat your offline one. As a matter of fact use the way you behave offline as a guide on how you now need to behave online.

Before semantic search came along you could safely assume that what happened on your website (or the social media network where you spent most time on), it stayed there. This is no longer the case. The web has become transparent. Data has become portable. By the same token the sense of authority and expertise you project have also become transparent and portable and that impacts directly upon your reputation. Reputation leads to trust. Without trust no business can ever take place. So developing a sense of trust in the online world is key to succeeding as a business.

Semantic Search Action List for #Step 1

1. Create a Google Account – go to: (http://**accounts.google**.com/)

2. Create a recognizable Gmail Address. Do not create anything spammy like MarketingGod@gmail.com – go instead for your name and experiment for ways that make it easy to remember. Think about how easy it will be to type it without making any spelling mistakes. This is particularly important if you have a name that is unusual or too long. You may want to experiment with ways to make it more user friendly.

3. Use Chrome as your web browser. I won't go into any detail here as it is covered in **Chapter 3**.

4. Allow Google to have access to your location (this is important for the quality of a number of Google services). Location-awareness in your Google account helps Google establish who you are and what you do a little faster. It has ramifications in a latter stage of search-promotional activity. I am assuming, here, that you will be actively involved in your website and online business promotion. If not, you can skip this, though it may be a good idea not to if you want to establish an online identity that Google search takes seriously.

5. Start thinking about what you need to do in order to establish as much "data density" as possible in your online presence. This includes thinking about the type of information you will put on your website and the kind of presence you will have to develop across the web, as a whole, through your social media profiles. Data density is not so much volume as consistency which can be easily cross-referenced. So, when you place, for instance, your address on your website and have an entirely different address where you do business on your LinkedIn account this creates ambiguity on the trustworthiness of the visible data about you, which affects how search assesses it.

6. You will need to think about shooting a couple of high-quality, head and shoulders shots of you. Approach this the same way you would offline: think in terms of the impression you want to create in your target audience when they see you for the first time. Also think in terms of "brand recognition". You want the visual of you to be clear and consistent. If possible, avoid the sunglasses look in avatars. You may think it is a cool look in real life but in the context of an online connection it only makes you look shifty.

7. In your Google Account you will need to set up Security (http://goo.gl/uN50Hu). This is really important. It is best if you set up two-step verification (http://goo.gl/ikveoX) and install Google Authenticator (http://goo.gl/cvl2Y) on your device(s). A hacking of your Google Account could seriously compromise everything you do online, just as identity theft can compromise your offline presence.

8. Set up backups. Link up and verify your cell phone to your Google account (if you haven't done so already) and put in place at least one more (if not two) alternative email addresses where you may be contacted.

9. Add a nickname. In the "Personal Info" section add a nickname you are known by, if applicable. This can be a pen name, if you are a writer, a stage name for an artist or actor or a name through which you are commonly associated with on forums.

10. In the "Languages" section of your Google account input any other languages that you understand. If you speak French or German, for instance, put that in there as well. Make sure that the information you place here is the same as with all other places where you are found (LinkedIn, Twitter etc).

Step #2

Establish your Identity

 # Establishing your identity is key in the semantic web.

Whether you are promoting yourself (as a microbrand) or your company as a full-blown brand the key requirements are the same. In order for you to establish your identity you need to take some practical steps.

Over time these may change a little so I will start with a brief explanation and a guiding principle. Semantic search works by joining up every piece of information it can find in order to form a picture of who you are. In this sense it is no different to how we have worked, since the beginning of time, as individuals, in the offline world. In order to achieve this goal semantic search requires a simple thing: data density which, really, should be called semantic density as data without connections and association to other data are very difficult to understand.

It's no longer enough to just 'be' online if you cannot also establish the credentials of who you are and what you do through the independent emergence of your name and brand on social media platforms, other publications perhaps, citations (if required) and as many favorable mentions as possible on the social web.

Whenever I mention this I get two reactions and they are both understandable: the first is a resistance to doing more work than is already being done, citing reasons of privacy, available resources and time. The second is the response that everything that can be done, is being done.

I understand the objections. None of them is an excuse and neither is entirely true, either. This is where the idea of semantic density comes in. In the offline world, because there is no real choice, we subconsciously do everything we do in a carefully considered way. The way we set up the physicality of a business, the buildings, décor, lighting, logo, colors, fonts and even merchandise positioning has a logic that resonates with the target audience.

In the offline world semantic density arises as a matter of course because we do not have to focus on the structure of the building, its building materials or the way the plumbers and electricians connected everything behind the scenes so that power flows along the wires and water runs from the taps. These are taken care of; for us, so we can focus on the things that really matter to our business.

Online, unfortunately, we acquire X-Ray vision. We see everything that is involved in the construction of our websites. When that happens it is distracting and it becomes difficult to know where to look at first. I have seen cases where website owners obsessed over getting pixels just right, trying to align banners and display items and then completely forget to address the real reason anyone would want to visit their website. Make sure then that its content, navigation, ease-of-use and the specific way it helps an online visitor do something they need to get done are at the center of your focus.

If you are setting up a website (or if you have one already) here are three things you should do to make sure it works the way it should:

1. **Check the Design.** Colors and pictures and clever scripts are great but they need to work to establish something specific that the target audience will appreciate because it helps them do what they want to do, more easily. If every design element on your website does not help guide the online visitor to do something that will help him or her, you may want to reconsider using it. If the way the website is set up visually does not immediately establish your brand and identity and appeal to the first-time visitor in an easy-to-understand way, you may want to reconsider some of its aspects. You really need to be ruthless here and choose to err on the side of function over art.

2. **Check the Content**. In the past you needed content because you needed content. The number of words (and by association the number of relevant words) played an important role in itself. As a result many websites ended up containing content that was thin in value but rich in keywords that were repeated in all their possible variations at every opportunity. Avoid this trap. The content you place on your website has to really work for your online visitors, delivering real value to them. Whether you're writing an "About Us" page or explaining something complicated, it really has to be unique in terms of tone and voice and explain exactly who you are. It also has to work in tandem with all the other copy you place on all the other pages so there is

no page where you will 'optimize' for landing and have copy elsewhere that does nothing or, worse still, works at odds with your 'best' pages.

3. Make it flat. Website architecture is something that's frequently overlooked. I've seen websites with great content that had it buried several levels deep and had, on top of that, failed to include a site search that would make content easier to find. The flatter your website structure is, the easier it becomes for the visitor to find what they are looking for and the easier a search engine spider indexes your site.

While the three steps detailed here seem to have little to do with identity they actually force you to think about how you want to work online. What is your 'style', what will drive your content creation, how will you project that? These are all identity questions.

Semantic Search Action List for #Step 2

1. Design your website to help your audience, not yourself. Your online success really depends on how good you are at being helpful to those who find you. Create a list of the questions and problems that trouble your target audience. Then assign design and content choices you have made on your website to the questions and problems of your audience. Do this right and you have a quick marketing win on your hands.

2. Plan before you write anything. Work out who your audience really is. Create content that answers the burning questions your audience has. Break down what you do in specific, related themes or one overarching theme (whichever is most suitable). Then use a thematic guide to help you be as detailed and thorough as possible in your content creation. This way you can create articles that can actually reference each other to provide greater depth on a particular question you are answering or a subject you are tackling.

3. Provide accessibility. Obstacles, however small, lose you customers and hurt your business. Streamline everything and work hard to understand where possible access obstacles reside in your website, your copy, the style of your communication, and so on. Then work to remove them.

4. Create a strategy before you do anything. I know it's basic but getting things done on the web takes time and effort. We all want to see a website being created and a business begin to work. Before you get to that stage take the time to think carefully why you're in business. What is it that drives you before the obvious need for money? Once you have that clear (and you will need to articulate it in writing) consider how you will make it clear to those who find you online.

5. Details are important. Put in as much data as possible about you and your business on the web. Do not forget to verify your business (if you are local) with Google: http://goo.gl/1xa5be

6. Decide on your communication style. Your tone and 'voice' become part of the character and personality your business develops. They help guide how others perceive you which guides their emotional response. This influences their willingness to connect with you.

7. Work from your strengths. While you really want to be everywhere on the web and do everything, you need to be realistic. At this early stage start off with what you are already good at and work on what you're not as you go on. Give yourself time to gain experience, and plan for the long haul.

8. Do not get locked into tunnels. Content is not just writing. It takes many different forms. Play to your strengths and start by producing content in ways that you are most comfortable with and confident in.

9. Remember there are people in your business. Nothing humanizes your business faster than pictures showing who the people behind it are. They do not have to be staged but they do have to appear somewhere.

10. Contact details. Do not make the mistake of leaving just an online form as the only means of contacting you. That's a very faceless way of reaching someone. Provide at least one more email address, provide a person's name, where necessary and a telephone number.

Step #3
Social Media

 # A strong social media presence is a powerful signal that search actually takes into account.

The impact a strong social media presence has on search (and SEO) is still being endlessly debated. It is, of course, the wrong question to ask. Those who look to a social media presence as a means of ranking quickly in search will be disappointed.

Social media is too unstructured and too unclear for Google (and other search engines) to take into account as a ranking signal. It is also too expensive, from a computer time perspective, to track, index, structure and keep tabs on all the time.

Yet, social media is very important. It provides social proof by way of interactions that can, in most cases, be independently corroborated by search. It creates a strong "social signature" that actually acquires value over time in terms of Google's E-A-T principle (Expertise, Authority and Trustworthiness) and it helps directly with brand recognition that is a requisite of trust in a brand.

As a matter of fact it would be entirely fair to day that the direct value of maintaining a strong social media presence to the webmaster or marketer is limited only by the limits of time, energy, commitment and imagination she is prepared to invest.

Discovering all the possible uses of social media activity however is something I will leave entirely up to you. What I will cover here are the more direct benefits a coherent social media profile provides you with and briefly explain the mechanics behind them.

I will start with a warning: Social media platforms are not yours. In some of the social media platforms (like Facebook and Instagram) the data you upload stops being yours the moment you upload it. Because you do not control the environment of any social media platform you should always use them in ways that directly help your brand and, where possible, lead back to your website.

That way, should something change in their programming or, should one of them close down for whatever reason you will not lose the brand value you have developed.

One further word of warning. Both Facebook and Instagram are walled gardens. What you do there; mostly stays there in the sense that search doesn't see it. This is why you need to also have an active presence on Twitter and LinkedIn even if the engagement you get on those platforms is way lower.

The Cover Shot

There are two photographs you need to take into account in most social media platforms. First your own photograph and second that of your background (also known as a Cover Shot) that will appear on your Profile page.

Choose a good quality personal photograph of yours as it will become part of your brand. Remember that people respond best to people photographs rather than cute animals, symbols or ideograms. A caricature might work but there has to be a point to it beyond "it's cute".

People you engage and interact with will use that photograph for instant, visual identification of who posted something or made a comment. Many of them will be on handheld devices so a photograph that's as clear as possible works best.

The background cover shot can be something evocative that you like or it can be something that you are promoting at the moment. It will serve you best if you make it something about who you are and what you do instead of an irrelevant picture.

You need to check the guidelines each social media platform puts out regarding the format, dimensions and size of the pictures you can upload there.

There are four distinct elements that are at play in most Cover Shots.

Fig. 3.1 - My Twitter cover photo provides four opportunities to communicate something to the viewer.

1. **Your name.** Make sure you're being consistent and also explore whether you can communicate additional information about you through it (you will have to Google the meaning of the parentheses around mine). If you're a business, use the brand name you're known by and again, think whether you can also express something of deeper value.

2. **Your background shot.** As you can see in this one I have chosen to use my Twitter cover shot to promote for a while, my book on decision making: *The Sniper Mind*. The book also tells the story about me: writer, that's corroborated by my bio.

3. **Your personal picture**. Try to make it as appealing as possible while also making it as close to who you are as you can.

4. **Where you work and where you live.** Both of these are signals which Google indexes and uses to understand who you are (important in semantic search) and what you do. It also uses it to divine context in your activities and search queries. It can become an important signal in terms of your authority across the web, in your chosen domain. You can put your website address on that line (as I have done).

In semantic search every detail counts. The clearer the information you put about yourself on the web, the better it is going to be from a search and branding point of view.

The About Section

Every social network has an "About" section. Each one is a little different but they're all designed to do the same thing: allow you to personalize the 'front window' of your social media profile on each social media platform.

There are three mistakes that are usually made here:

1. The essay bio that starts from the first year in Junior school onwards.

2. The cutesy bio that tries to stand out from the crowd by being sassy or street smart hoping

that those who read it will remember it and engage.

3. The faceless bio that puts in buzzwords like "passion", "focus", "guru", "ninja" that ultimately mean nothing.

Your bio in each social media profile is an opportunity to be human, project what is really important to you and give those who have taken the time to read it, the opportunity to get to know you a little better.

I know the competition is fierce and the temptation to try for a strong first impression is often irresistible. Resist it you must however if you want to be true to who you are.

The easiest example I can give you here is my own Twitter bio which reads: *Author, Speaker, Analyst. Contributor @Inc. Represented by The Knight Agency. Latest book: "The Sniper Mind". Political at times out of conviction not ideology.*

It's just 22 words long. It took me about four days of thinking and writing and deleting to put together and despite it being so short is actually has five distinct sections each of which represents a part of who I am, what I do and the values that drive me.

I will break it down for you so you can see the process I went through when I was writing it.

Section 1 – The tag line. "Author, Speaker, Analyst" appears virtually everywhere on the web in relation to me. It is listed in that order on all my profiles and that is also how I appear at interviews. The three words explain the order of what I do for a living and the importance of each of these activities in my professional life. They give an instant flavor of who I am to those who have never heard of me and help those who know me and read my many different types of articles or listen to me on interviews, better understand and clarify in their minds what I do.

Section 2 – The CV. It is always hard to decide what to include by way of professional qualifications and achievements. In third grade I came first at shot put. If this was relevant I would have put it there. As it is, I had to think that my audience on Twitter is a mix between people who know me and people who decide to follow me because of articles they're read, books they've bought or talks they have attended. My CV needs to reinforce in their minds that they're not making a mistake by following me. Plus it is intended to help them understand that I truly am who I am. Anyone can say "hey I am a writer." Writing for Inc.com is difficult unless you are an experienced writer and/or an authority in your field. Of all the many magazines, websites and blogs I contribute to Inc.com has strong recognition to the business audience and it is a little edgy which is why I chose it.

Section 3 – Authority. Anyone can call themselves a writer these days. That's the easy part. Having a prestigious Agency represent you is way harder. It means you are a writer who sells. This section was the easiest choice I had to make and yet it only occurred to me after days of thinking. Including it here adds gravity to what comes afterwards. It also serves to mark me in the mind of the visitor to my profile as that rarity: a published, professional author who makes his living out of writing.

Section 4 – The ask. Should someone read my profile, I reasoned, there should be an opportunity for them to access some of the things I do. In this particular occasion this focused on my latest book on decision making: *The Sniper Mind*. Not only does this reinforce pretty much everything that I have placed in my profile so far but it also closes the visual cue loop supplied by my choice of cover shot.

Section 5 – Me. The final words on my profile humanize me a little, render me vulnerable and also allow the casual visitor to my profile to understand me a little better. It is true I Tweet about politics on both sides of the Atlantic. All my Tweets reflect my own personal values and commitment to greater equality in society and greater social justice. In that sense they are not party political even if they happen to represent something posted by a party.

And that's it. You can hopefully see the amount of work that went into those 22 words. It was the thinking and experimentation behind it that actually made it happen.

A similar five section approach should be applied to each of the social media profiles you populate. The tone and values reflected in each should be an extension of your website and the brand that you are building.

This works the same way as an individual building a personal brand and a company that is focused on branding its business. The scale will obviously be a little different and the time required to achieve good quality branding will reflect that. The underlying, basic principles that guide the process however are exactly the same.

Personal or Business?

The question of whether it is better to promote and brand a business as a business or to work through a personal account is easier to answer than most people think.

If you're a solopreneur, a writer, artist, content creator and so on then really it is you who is the brand. It is you that you need to focus on, explain to your audience and build up.

This will not dilute your efforts in terms of content sharing and content creation activities and it will definitely help you make the most of the limited resources of time available to you.

Marketing of any kind on a social media platform is driven by interaction and engagement. Because people most readily react to and engage with people, a Personal Profile will always find it easier to gain traction and generate engagement than a Business Page which, inevitably, is there to primarily market to people rather than engage in the sharing of opinion or thought.

This leads us rather neatly to the question of if you do have a business profile how do you use it to market effectively?

Marketing with a Business Profile

Marketing effectively, in a semantic web, revolves around those three 'little' requirements: Trust, Authority, Reputation. People like doing business with people, Authority and Reputation are a lot more easily gained if you are a person as opposed to a faceless business with a logo. The only time this is not true is if you already have a brand in place that is globally known and which has a massive advertising budget to put behind its message.

This does not mean that your business profile should throw to the wind every principle of marketing and start to share content that falls outside its business remit, or engage in conversations like a person. Quite the opposite in fact.

Your business profile, being a page about business, should share content that is original and business focused. Your business page cover photo, for instance, should be updated to reflect seasonal or time-sensitive promotions. Your posts should be, mostly, during business hours and be 100% about business.

Sound as it may be however this strategy on its own will not get your business profile many followers. Without followers it will not get the eyeballs it needs in order to generate business or build brand value.

Breaking the impasse is where your personal Profile comes in. A business is owned by a person. A business has some employees who work in it. Social media profiles that are related to a business can (and should) share at least some of the content of the business profile they are affiliated with. They are the real experts who can quantify the importance of particular posts shared by the business, in their introduction of the share.

They are also the ones who can talk, intelligently, about what a business does without sounding like an advert for it. A personal social media profile that shares some of the content of the social media business profile should be part of the strategy of establishing the real Unique Selling Proposition of the business and its activities.

Approached like this, within any social media platform, you are able to leverage both the presence of personal profiles and the business profile in the best possible way.

Semantic Search Action List for Step #3

1. Create a list of your brand values. Use value words like “fair”, “positive”, “engaging”, “playful” etc to craft a profile of your brand’s character.

2. Make a list of all the social media platforms in which your brand has a presence. Determine what type of content will reflect your brand values in each platform.

3. Create a reasonable schedule for posting content on each platform. List why you think the times you have picked are the best to post content.

4. Make a list of all the problems your product or service solves for your audience.

5. Match your words from point one of this list with the words from point four. Decide if there is a match or a clash. Adjust the words from point one to reflect the tone that is best required by what you do.

6. Decide your tone when posting content or sharing content in your social media accounts. Is the company serious or playful? Is it reserved and aloof or super-friendly and engaging?

7. Take four pictures that reflect your brand values and match the tone you use to communicate through your social media accounts.

8. Detail how you plan to tie in seasonal and one-off promotions of your business with the business and personal profiles. How will you get your employees to share or engage in a way that maintains your brand values and image?

9. Shoot a 30-second video that reflects what you do and showcases at least one of your brand values. Detail how you will use it and what small adjustments you will need to make in the way you introduce it on each different social media platform.

10. Explain what you expect to see of your website content in Google search; because of your social media activity.

Step #4
Entities and Graphs

 # Google is mining the web looking to connect the dots of your digital identity.

Semantic search is a holistic effort by Google (primarily) to understand who you are and what you do across the web. This guide is essentially all about that and provided you put into effect each of the 20 steps detailed in this book you will have a higher visibility on the web, regardless of whether you understand the theory behind semantic search or not.

If you do want to delve a little deeper in the different ways Google finds out who you are and creates a cohesive picture of your digital identity, here's a link you can follow: http://goo.gl/Lv5Lmf.

Google is busy building entities. An entity, whether a person or a thing, requires the independent collection of facts about them and a cross-referencing of these facts through their digital footprint.

This becomes an exercise in digital identity building that is based on the trustworthiness of the information provided. Put bluntly the more Google can see consistency in the activity and general interests across all your digital profiles, the more likely it is to think you are a real person (as opposed to a spammer) with real interests and some kind of authority and expertise.

Fig. 4.1 - A Google search for David Amerland provides the familiar Knowledge Graph box with the social media profiles associated with the person, displayed.

If, as a person or a company, you are building a brand then Google's ability to "connect the dots" of who you are and what you do is key to your being able to stand out in search.

Semantic search requires three things: Trust, Authority and Reputation. All three revolve around your digital profiles, their activity and the sentiment levels and engagement that each generates. Semantic search also requires differentiation – the ability of search to understand the "uniqueness" of you.

Standing out in search is not that difficult if your name happens to be Charisma Carpenter (named after an Avon perfume), Charlize Theron or Chord Overstreet but what if you happen to be named Joe Smith or Janet Williams? These are names which produce hundreds, possibly thousands of results of different people.

Search can deliver the 'right' Joe Smith or Janet Williams to the right person provided it knows who Joe Smith and Janet Williams really are, what they like, what they share, where they are, who they know, what's their subject expertise and what it is they do. You can make that process easier by cross-linking to your digital profiles, when possible (i.e. mentioning them on your website, your social media profile page, linking back to your website from each of them, when possible, etc) and you could, even begin to change your profile name so that there is consistency across all your digital profiles.

That. Of course, is not enough. It is not enough for you to just tell Google who you are and what you do, you must also show it through your online activity.

8. **Charisma Carpenter**
Actress, The Disposable

Born July 23, 1970, in Las Vegas, Charisma Carpenter was named after an Avon perfume (a fact that did not sit well with her). She studied classical ballet from age five. Her family moved around often. As a youngster, she entered many local beauty contests, and attended Gorman High School in Las Vegas...

9. **Charlize Theron**
Actress, Prometheus

Charlize Theron was born in Benoni, a city in the greater Johannesburg-area, in South Africa, the only child of Gerda Theron (née Maritz) and Charles Theron. She was raised on a farm outside the city. Theron is of Afrikaner (Dutch, with some French Huguenot and German) descent, and Afrikaner military figure Danie Theron was her great-great-uncle...

10. **Chord Overstreet**
Actor, The Hole

Chord Overstreet was born in Nashville, Tennessee, to Julie (Miller), a make-up artist, and Paul Overstreet, a country musician and songwriter whose own father was a pastor. Chord and his five siblings were raised in a creative and music-filled environment, with their father highly involved in the music industry. His brother, Nash Overstreet, is in the band Hot Chelle Rae...

Fig. 4.2 - Although they did not probably plan it this way, these Hollywood stars have a distinct, competitive advantage when it comes to branding and search.

Showing who you are is harder to fake because it takes a lot more effort than just telling search who you are. If you are known, for example, as an arts expert inevitably you will talk about art in some of your digital profiles in ways that will elicit specific responses and engagement from those you interact with.

Google sees these conversations. The data that gets mined are the profiles you regularly engage with, the repeat factor of your interactions, the nature of those interactions, the length of the comments in each interaction, the sentiment of those interactions and the subsequent behavior after the interaction is over.

Filling in all these blanks and helping Google join the dots has two distinct effects: First it begins to create a certain amount of "data density" in your online activity. Second it helps others who may not have come across you and your business before, discover you through different platforms. This leads to a double-win. You get to expand the size of your online audience while gaining traction in semantic search, at the same time.

It requires a certain amount of planning, thinking and discipline. This is not the kind of activity you can do in stops and starts. It does need you to have a sustained and sustainable strategy in place.

Although I have used the word "strategy" here, really, your digital activity across all your digital profiles should constitute a clear digital footprint that should clearly reflect your business identity.

Graph Activity

As you've gathered from this chapter, in addition to entities Google is also building graphs. A graph is a map that shows the relationship between two or more quantities or two or more entities.

Graphs become the ultimate differentiation factor. In my previous example of "Janet Williams" the search for her becomes difficult only if we have no graph to work with. Then all women named Janet Williams in the world; who happen to be online become equally viable as a result.

If, however, we are searching for Janet Williams, secretary of the year in Albuquerque the search narrows down considerably. This is true even if Janet Williams herself did not put out an online announcement to the world that she'd become secretary of the year in that particular metropolitan area.

How? Online activity is an integral part of our individual identity curation effort. In my Janet Williams example someone she's already friends with would have noticed her achievement. It would have come up in her online conversations and congratulations would have been exchanged. Maybe some local trade publication or a company newsletter would have cited it, in which case it would have been reshared by those closest to her, at least. And search engines would have noticed too.

If the Janet Williams we are looking for had also happened to Tweet about this and provide a link to her company's website mentioning her achievement our search would be over very quickly. But nothing is ever as simple as that.

First, there is the graph we generate. A perfect stranger searching for a perfect stranger is about as close as we get to the search equivalent of a needle in a haystack. People likely to search for the Janet Williams of my example are connected to her in some way (friends, High School classmates, co-workers, etc) or are looking in her related area (researchers compiling "secretary of the year" results, for instance). The real point is nothing happens in a vacuum and, somewhat mystically, nothing happens without a reason.

This brings us back to graph mining. Google's efforts in this area seek to better understand the intent behind each search and the intent in each search query.

A graph may be an evaluated list of the connections between people, objects, events and facts but it is also a dynamic, evolving thing. No search engine is going to store trivia forever. If our Janet Williams has her 15 minutes of fame on the web and then goes on and has a brilliant, happy, quiet life where she never again posts anything of meaning our ability to find her through search will become exponentially harder if not impossible.

The news about her won't be recent. The connections with people and news sites and events will be progressively weakened and she, as a person of importance in the secretarial achievement awards world, will drop out of Google's Index and be lost to our ability to digitally find her, forever.

All this is a crass, broad strokes, example that glosses over many fine technical points and presents some deep, sweeping assumptions on how people engage and interact online and how Google indexes their data.

As such, however, I hope it helps you understand immediately the importance of ongoing online activity as a means of building a brand and maintaining its visibility in Google search by continuing to make it feel relevant. To achieve this you need to have in place a workable digital marketing and content production strategy you can implement on a day-to-day basis.

Semantic Search Action List for Step #4

1. Articulate the aim of your marketing and content creation efforts. Use words that reflect the values of your brand and help answer the questions your audience has about your products or services.

2. Create a spreadsheet that lists all your social media channels. Now beneath each one allocate each of the value words that describes your brand.

3. Sticking with the same spreadsheet of action point two, now list specific themes you can use to group your content sharing or content creation efforts. Allocate the themes you have come up with to specific social media channels.

4. Again, sticking with the same spreadsheet you started in action point two, list the kinds or types of photographs that showcase the brand values you have listed or are in keeping with your brand's identity.

5. Now identify the major online influencers who are active in your industry.

6. Make a short list of the influencers whose activities and output best represent your brand values and attitude.

7. Create a plan to engage, reshare and interact with the industry influencers you have identified as helpful to your brand. Decide what activities of yours will also be beneficial to them and could create the starting point of a mutually beneficial relationship.

8. Reinforce the digital presence of those who share your content by resharing their shares.

9. Tag people online and credit them with the content you share or the ideas their activities spark.

10. Create a daily routine of low-effort posts; the sharing of pictures, memes, video snippets or other people's content that is relevant to your brand.

Step #5

Content

 # Content is now key to your website's visibility, your branding and the creation of your digital identity

Everything you see in the world around you is content of some kind. The clothes you wear, the songs you sing, the ads you watch, the food you buy, the tunes you hum and the memes you share. Everything is a signal that sends a message.

As a matter of fact, in the 'real world' (and I am using the inverted commas knowingly) we're all expert transmitters of messages that announce our interests, status, and intent and we're extremely adept in burying within each one of our transmissions the subtext of our status and the scope of our mission.

All of the things we do constitute a signal that gets decoded the moment someone relevant to us, looks at us with intent, otherwise it appears to be just so much background noise.

The only reason we can function at all in such an environment lies in our magnificently complex brains and their ability to process an incredible amount of information subconsciously (up to 40 million bits each second, apparently) while our conscious minds can barely crawl along at just 40 bits per second.

The reason this is important is that in the digital world, whether you are marketing, burning time or just learning the ropes, you need to be every bit as real as in the 'real' world in order to have any kind of identity that stands out from the general noise.

Creating a signal of who you are also establishes your credentials in the fullest possible sense of the word. This is an opportunity, as well as a challenge and content is key to it.

What Kind of Content?

The obvious question I get asked a lot at corporate meetings is "what kind of content should we produce?" I always find it incredible when I talk to executives working in Fortune 500 companies to hear them suggest that not that much is happening behind their companies' office walls.

The problem here is that usually too much is happening, rather than not enough but it becomes absorbed in the everyday routine of doing "business as usual" to the degree that it fails to appear newsworthy or even worth mentioning.

This is a blind spot that every business develops with time and you will have to work hard to overcome it. In the semantic web content is your identity the same way your clothes, voice, accent and behavior, contextually define who you are in the offline world. This means that when it comes to thinking about content; text, photographs, Tweets, blogposts, Press Releases, website design change decisions and videos are all in the game.

Ideally, a mid-size business or even a single-person, working from home, has to be: an expert writer, a great photographer, a videographer, a director (and lighting expert), a social media guru and a professional publicist and that's before we touch upon the need for domain knowledge, industry insights and the occasional exclusive post that grabs and leads the online conversation.

Or, you can just be you. Forget about the medium and think instead about the message. Forget about the clever stylistics, the professional twirls that allow one to manipulate the emotion of the audience and think, instead, how can you serve best those you want to do business with. What burning questions do they have about your products or services that they would like to have answered?

That is your "content strategy". Sure, we can talk about trends and "twelve month plans" and the need to newsjack in order to get a coattail ride on a fast-moving story, but none of these techniques and ploys will do you any good if your content sucks.

Do you want to be a trustworthy, credible entity on the web? One that is seen as having some authority? It's easy. Make sure your content has real value.

The only way to do this is to make sure that it really answers vital questions your audience has that need answering. In many ways you'll be served best if you forget about marketing completely and rekindle your passion for your business. Rediscover the reason you got in business in the first place. When you have done that all that remains is for you to find ways to get that across to your target audience.

People love to do business with passionate people and no one likes a drone. It's easy, I hope, to see which one you (and your business) need to be.

Content and Blogging

The social media web is a very noisy one indeed and making sure that you are heard requires you to shout more effectively, rather than louder. This is where your blog really earns its keep.

The way this works is simple:

- Create content that is of real, direct value to your online visitors.
- Make your content easy to access across different devices and screen resolutions.
- Make your content easy to share across different social networks.

The content you create and then share is part of your digital identity. It helps those who consume it to understand who you are, why you do the things you do and what values you stand for. As a result content is the primary means through which you establish your online identity, create your reputation and generate the all essential sense of trust without which nothing else can take place.

To do all this you need to have in place:

- Consistency in your content subject matter, tone of communication and frequency of posting.
- Authenticity in the content you post.
- Authority in your subject matter.

You know that your content is working when it delivers online visitor interaction by way of approval (usually through a positive response on a social media platform) and re-sharing and engagement (usually by way of commenting).

All of these are activities that have an incremental impact on the ranking of your content, and therefore your website, in Google's search.

When you create content for your website you should be going through all these steps anyway which begs the question, if you want to attract search engine attention is there anything else you should be doing?

Well, yes. You should check out both LinkedIn and Twitter, each day and see what is trending in each social network. If you discover something that resonates with what you do you should write about it.

Both Twitter and LinkedIn offer the use of hashtags and you should be using them when you create content around trending topics.

One small word of caution when you do this. Make sure that the content you create fits in with what you do. Content that jars. Content that brings traffic to your website but does not fit in with everything else you do may work against you, creating a negative image of who you are and what your business does.

Two Types of Content To Keep in Mind

Within the web there are two types of content you need to be aware of and your content creation efforts should tackle both on an, at least, 80/20 split.

The first type of content is called 'Evergreen'. You should aim to make this the bulk of your content creation. The second type of content is 'Topical'. This is where the content inspired by trending topics falls in. Topical content has the ability to really bring in large numbers of visitors, quickly but it then peters out fast.

Evergreen content, as the name suggests, works for all time, all the time. It may not bring thousands of visitors to your blog, each day, but overall it is a solid performer that constantly adds value to your website.

Because "evergreen' content never stops working, as a strategy it should be part of the increasing visibility drive of a website's maturity on the web. There is a proviso however and it is called relevance.

Older content that is relevant and older content that is evergreen still has to feature in your content promotion schedule so that it can be rediscovered. Search engines and Google, in particular, use the engagement signals of those who see it as one small part of their on-going assessment of its value.

In addition, where possible, older content should be updated either by adding relevant links to fresh content that complements it, or adding new references and studies, where appropriate.

Keep in mind that when you create content you are addressing search queries as opposed to single keywords. This means that you need to think about the intent behind the query, especially as you create 'Evergreen' content.

It is admittedly harder than just addressing keywords but it works out a lot better for you in the long run.

One other question which has come up in relation to using a blog is the length of each blog post. Now there is no real hard and fast rule here. Google has, over the years, through the announcements of Matt Cutts, who is head of its web spam team, mentioned that longer blog posts as opposed to shorter ones signal that you have taken some trouble in its creation and some thought in its writing, as opposed to throwing up some rubbish you typed up quickly.

Longer, in this case is over four hundred words in length but that is a guideline as opposed to an iron-clad rule. Shorter content that has a bit of punch and generates engagement is just as important. So rather than getting hung up on the fact that Google likes longform writing, make the decision based on what's best for the subject you are covering and for the readers you are addressing.

If the subject matter demands 1,500 words then go for it. If however you only need 250 to do it justice, then stretching the length is a disservice to those who will come to read it and it will boomerang on you, eventually.

Within this thought it is also worth to consider the fact that many in your target audience will be short on time and unable to habitually devote a lot of time reading longform writing. What they usually need is a quick read that will give them something of value they can use as they go about their busy lives.

Ten Decisions You Have to Make as a Blogger

The first thing to bear in mind is that when it comes to your blog, like any other kind of business or online presence, you are in complete control. The direction you take will depend upon inclination, skills, resources and goals. The steps which follow are the critical ones you now need to make as a blogger in order to ensure you end up with a blog that fulfils you as well as its intended audience.

01. Decide your focus. The days when you could have a blog that would cover everything imaginable and still rank well on Google because of its sheer size are now over. What you need to do is specialize in one core area with perhaps a tangential subject or two which you use either to increase your range and provide variety or really need it in order to provide greater depth. This works if you are running a business as well as if you are running a blog that's mainly intended to get traffic and bring you advertising. It also means that quality now trumps size, every single time.

02. Create authority. If you are not in total control of your subject you may still get by, by doing your research and synthesizing a point of view which is unique. Authority in writing now has as much to do with what's fresh and new as what is truly knowledgeable. The latter can be bought in through careful research but without the former you will only end up rehashing what's already 'out there' and that will not get you very far.

03. Set the tone. Personalisation has become crucial. You may be a one-man outfit or you may actually be running a 300-person company, if you cannot talk to your online visitors like they are real people and like you are a real person you have lost a vital opportunity to make a human connection.

04. Decide the frequency. Ideally you should write every day. That may work if you are a writer but even seasoned writers find it hard to sustain that kind of output. So decide what works for you and stick to it. It is more important, from a search engine point of view to create a regularity than to be erratic. It is more important from a visitor point of view to have something to say which truly needs to be said than to be prolific. Think and act strategically here.

05. Provide value. Value is at the core of everything you do online. There has been a gradual but noticeable shift in the way online visitors access information. Hardly anyone reads these days. They quickly check the site, scan the article and will only give you their time if you have given them something which has truly gripped their attention and can now hold it so they can learn something of value. Value has a lot to do with everything we discussed so far. It is determined by the focus of your writing, it helps create authority on your website, it can be influenced by the tone of what you say and it can then decide the frequency of what you write.

06. Get interactive. Forget the traditional perception of some magical divide on the other side of which was 'them'. Now the entire web is 'us'. Your writing no longer takes place from a pulpit, aimed at an audience. It is more like a conversation started with the person next to you. So make sure you have in place a commenting system for people to respond through (and monitor it) and provide social sharing buttons so they can use your content to comment on social media networks.

07. Be real. There is a strong temptation to play it safe online. To avoid saying the obvious or voicing what you think because you really do not want to upset anybody. However there is a very clear difference between being intentionally controversial for controversy's sake and writing about something you feel strongly about. If you do truly feel strongly about a subject and have the evidence to back it up, then have the guts to write about it. Social media (of which your blog is now part of) works as a concept because it is real and tries hard to stay honest.

08. Listen to your readers. Respond to comments. Answer emails and comment back on social networks when readers interact with your posts. You may be the originator of your writing but in many ways writing has become a collaborative exercise. Those who take the time to read what you write feel that they also have an opinion about it which deserves to be listened to, and they are right. The best online content is created in response to the interests of its readership.

09. Invest time in your writing. Think carefully who you are writing for. Way too frequently writers make assumptions about their audience in regards to knowledge and interests that are inaccurate and it leads to gaps in the writing itself which could have been avoided if a little more time had been invested in creating the post. If you are challenged for time to write do not try to fit it into ten minute slots where you bang out some writing quickly. That is more likely to be the kind of writing which is easy to dismiss and you don't really want to go there.

10. Put yourself out there. You could be a plumber or a rocket scientist, you still need to try and find where your audience is. If you are not part of a social network, have a presence in forums or are present in professional associations, online, you are missing an opportunity to interact with your target audience.

The social media web requires content and Google's use of machine learning in search has made real content, with real value to its audience, the only solution to being noticed by search. This brings us to the felicitous situation of being able to increase website rankings mostly with writing. But the writing has to be of the sort that provides a solution to an online visitor's problem with the friendly, casual tone you would expect to hear in a face to face meeting with a friend.

Semantic Search Action List for Step #5

1. Look again at the brand values you listed in Step #3 of this book (if you're not following the steps sequentially, now's a good time to look at that step). Take five photographs that reflect those brand values.

2. From the five photographs you took that reflect your brand values pick out the ones that also project your marketing message. If none do you will need to rethink your marketing or reconsider your brand values.

3. Write down five light-hearted or even playful, positive messages you could Tweet on Twitter that reflect your brand values or brand personality.

4. List the theme or themes that reflect the nature of your business and brand. Remember the theme is always bigger than your products and services.

5. Write a Tweet you can use to promote one of your brand values. Now expand this Tweet into a paragraph that could be used to start a blog post. Now also take one picture you could use to represent the same brand value.

6. What selection process did you use to complete point five above? Detail your thinking in a paragraph that can be used as a guide to do this for all your other brand values and marketing messages.

7. List your social media channels in descending order of engagement.

8. Match the social media channels you listed in point seven above with the brand values you project most in each one. Can you see which one resonates the most with your audience? Do you understand why?

9. Describe the tone that best fits the way you communicate with Tweets, social media posts, blogs and pictures. Is it "straight, but playful", "sincere and professional" etc.

10. List all the value words that best fit what you've described in point nine above. For instance: "fun", "jargon-free", "direct", "simplified", etc. See if the words themselves tell a story about your business and brand.

Step #6
Voice Search

 # Voice search is changing the way data surfaces on search because it changes both search query and intent

Here's a truth: despite the fact that I first wrote about the impact of voice search in the first edition of *Google Semantic Search* in 2012 its quality, though improved, still leaves much to be desired.

Here's another truth: its usage grows every year. It is driven by form (i.e. the extensive use of smart speakers and voice-operated smart devices) rather than function. And it is changing the way searches are carried out by introducing imprecise, natural language queries that require additional, contextual data to define correctly.

Understand this now: Voice search will eventually become the dominant method of input query in search far outstripping the forty eight per cent plus, of general web search queries that it holds now. But it will take time.

What's holding it back in no particular order are:

1. Difficulties in ascertaining context in the search query.

2. Difficulties in disambiguation in the search query.

3. The psychological shift in using spoken words to look for information in an answer that will be spoken back to us.

You can take it as a given that points one and two are technological hurdles that will be overcome relatively quickly. The third one however is a biological one.

Consuming information by voice is tricky. We simply cannot retain a lot of factual information when it is spoken back to us. As a result we tend to ask for things we expect to have a relatively short answer or even a "yes" or "no" answer such as: "Will it rain today?" or "Is it hot outside?" Or things that are sufficiently contextual for us to retain the gist of the spoken information without a lot of effort.

So, voice search queries tend to be either short and to the point or, sometimes, longer but with the expectation that the answer will be light on information.

Because of all this voice searches, according to statistics released by Google, are thirty per cent more likely to be searches leading to some action.

Before we go further let's tackle the two questions that consistently pop up in relation to voice search:

1. Can I optimize my website for voice search?

2. Does Google use a separate Voice Search Index?

The answer to the first question is yes you can but that is part of your overall SEO efforts instead of specifically focusing for voice search.

Achieving data density in your content, clarity, usefulness, authority and trustworthiness are the keys to benefiting from voice search.

The answer to the second is no. Google uses the same index it uses for global web search to deliver results in voice search through its mobile devices and home assistants.

Voice search answers to search queries do tend to be different to web searches some times but that is because of the different technology Google uses at the voice search interface.

Home assistants and digital assistants on mobile devices use a host of natural language processing (NLP) algorithms, alongside data pulled from the device location, search history of the user, digital profile and so on to better understand the context of spoken search queries.

At some point in the future this will be refined further to gauge sentiment by recognizing urgency in the voice and so on. Despite all this, spoken search queries are often vague and imprecise and this makes them hard to recognize.

Like everything else that has to do with search the onus to take action is on you: the website owner, the SEO, the entrepreneur, the business owner.

It is you who has to make sure your business and its website can be found when needed through the best organization and optimization of data possible.

Structured data plays a key role here but that is not the only requirement, and we shall get to structured data on Step #7 of this book.

Semantic Search Action List for Step #6

1. Make sure you have a Frequently Asked Questions (FAQs) page on your website. The answers you provide have to be clear, useful and as comprehensive and on-point as possible.

2. Compile a list of questions about your business that a customer would ask about it from voice search. Once you do, consider, does your website really answer them?

3. Compile a list of questions about your business that a customer would ask from voice search if he or she didn't really know what your business does. Does your website really answer *them*?

4. If you serve a particular geographic location consider how would your business show up on a mobile device?

5. Are directions to your business easy to find? Are opening hours and a contact number easy to find?

6. Has your website layout been designed to be as accessible to search as possible? Is there a relatively flat structure and a good cross-linking strategy that helps content be discovered by search? Is Javascript, if any, implemented correctly?

7. Make sure the content you create adds depth to the main subject matter(s) of your website. Keep your syntax structure short and conversational.

8. Keep track of the content you create and start to cross-linking pages so that you add additional value to their content by linking to other pages on your website that have additional content on the same subject.

9. Do not be afraid to link to authoritative, external sources that add additional value to the content you create.

10. Check each page of content you create to see if it answers specific questions concisely and clearly. Always carry out this check when you create fresh content.

Step #7
Structured Data

 # Structured data helps search engines understand content better and it makes indexing easier.

Semantic search and the semantic web are all about structured data.

Google is busy indexing the unstructured web (which is most websites and social media content) and turning it into structured data inside its index.

The moment we talk semantic search we are basically talking meaning: ways and means to derive signal from all the noise. This requires content and context. And both need to be understood by search in order for this to work.

Just as the mind looks at the world, collects a ton of apparently useless detail and then sifts through it adding meaning (some irrelevant piece of information overheard in a conversation between two strangers, acquires different context when coupled with additional knowledge regarding a particular incident at their locale, for example) so does search, index the largely unstructured web, collecting information and then bringing it back to be structured so that it can acquire meaning.

There are two implicit statements in this: First, that the information itself can be understood so that it can then be accurately related to other bits of information. Second, that in making connections between different bits of information there is a way to sift through what's true and what's false and draw inferences from both.

This is where structured data comes in. The primary worry most webmasters have is that the application of structured data (which can be hard to do) becomes a ranking signal in search, that they miss out on.

On that score let's clarify that Google uses existing structured data it finds to better understand a web page but does not rank that web page any different to any similar web page that does not have structured data. To put this in a different way, provided there is equally good value between two web pages of which only one has structured data implemented on it, there is no difference in the way Google will look at them. There is one more proviso I will add here to this equivalence: clarity.

The implementation of structured data is intended to make content on web pages clearer and easier for search engines to understand. This implies that many times the wording, structure and context of what we write on the web is not immediately obvious to search.

That's your cue for the one, constant guideline you need every time you create content of any type: Clarity.

Ask yourself: does it fit in with my brand? Does it reflect my business? Does it depict the character and voice my business has developed? Is it immediately recognizable as my own?

Each of these questions will have a slightly different answer but in their totality they should all point to the same thing: brand building. Brand building requires a singular focus on brand message. To stick brand message requires values. Values require a clearly worked out identity.

This is where it gets real. If you're reading this book by dipping in, Step #2 tackles the practicalities of building an identity. An identity though is a lot more than just the design of your website or the message you put out in your social media channels.

A sense of identity means that your business, your brand knows what it stands for, it understands its values and purpose and it these values and purpose that guide the practicality of doing business.

Implementing structured data markup (and the W3C organization has a full page describing the application and format of semantic markup: http://goo.gl/IZwVkz) is not a shortcut that will work if you fail to have true clarity in your content and a brand with a real identity.

This entire book, more or less, is all about helping your website get indexed in a structured way that helps it define its authority and uniqueness on the web. So if you follow all the steps in here and do nothing active about implementing structured markup, you should still be OK as far as search indexing and visibility are concerned.

The key to everything is as simple to detail as it is hard to do well:

- Careful planning beforehand
- Consistency in the style of execution
- Sustainability in the overall execution
- A willingness to be as real as possible in how you operate

Structured Data or Structured Content?

When it comes to content search engines and human visitors want the same things:

- Context
- Relevance
- Clarity

Until relatively recently newspapers and magazines struggled with the web. The content which they depended on, to bring out their stories was either freely available directly from the source or was also being produced by countless rivals. In addition content that they had to bring out to justify their presence was either incredibly time-consuming to produce (which made it expensive) or soaked up manpower and resources that should have been spent elsewhere.

Journalism is evolving and in its evolution, we also see how businesses that also need to produce content, can use best practice to do more, with less.

Associated Press (AP) and the BBC are about as far apart in terms of what each does as you can possibly imagine. One processes an incredible amount of raw information by way of leads and stringer reports that needs to be written up quickly and effectively and fed to news outlets, while the other does the same but packages its content to be consumed by its own public. In terms of audience the first one is a B2B business while the second is a B2C.

While each has a very specific niche and a clearly defined audience there is a significant audience overlap for both, created by the fact that on the web, everything is accessible to everybody. To make matters even more complex the Associated Press, in a typical B2B set up, operates out of a website while the BBC runs a 'shop' in terms of its televised content.

Both organizations face:

- Increased pressure in terms of lead time for news as the web moves ever faster
- Increased competition from bloggers and citizen journalists
- A struggle to retain audience attention across the distractions offered by the social web
- A need to reduce operational costs to maintain the viability of their business model

- A drive to remain relevant in order to maintain their respective market position

Both use technology to address all of this but each does it very differently. The difference is instructive and directly applicable to your own efforts to create a sustainable web presence through content creation.

Structured Data and Automation

Associated Press has gone down the structured data, automated route. One large slice of AP work is processing and then releasing company earnings reports. The flow of data here is constant. The work tedious and very detail-orientated, requiring a high degree of accuracy with figures and, it has to be said, mind-numbingly boring for a trained journalist.

By using algorithms that take highly structured data and produce stories on items such as the net income and sales of public companies AP has managed to:

- Increase the number of stories it brought out per quarter from 300 to over 3,700 – an increase of 1,200% with a further 127% productivity gain expected by the end of this year.

- Free up to 20% of journalists' time that can now be applied on stories where the human factor is indispensable.

- Broaden the reach of its brand by creating more relevant content than ever before.

- Maintain its market lead by simply being present in more reports, social conversations and news outlets than ever, because of its increased output

Content That's Highly Structured

The BBC has gone down the path where it takes highly unstructured content and filters it to create relevance and context, therefore transforming it into a story that provides for its audience context and relevance and helps deliver real meaning.

To do this it uses the usual trope of a news presenter but instead of just reading the news and being reduced to speculation when news stories are breaking, he (in this case) provides a bird's eye-view of the context of the story and its impact by pulling in outside sources from across the web in real time on a news board.

The *BBC Outside Source Program* uses a structured approach to curation

This way events happening across social media and the blogosphere that impact on current news story in a way that is yet hard to see can be contextualized and become part of the story themselves. The result is that content that is highly unstructured in nature is curated in a way that allows the BBC, televised news report to remain compelling in the age of the web.

Both companies do something unique. They use content that can be found across the web and process it in a way that allows both to rise above their competitors. AP through speed of processing and the sheer volume of reports it puts out which make it the go-to hub for news information, for news outlets. The BBC through clever interlinking.

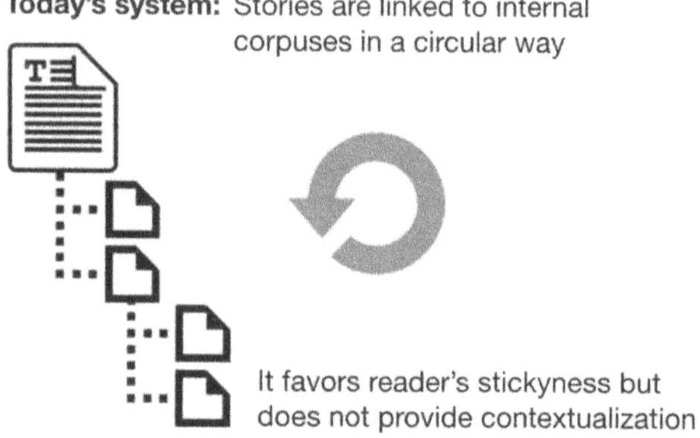

Fig. 7.1 - Linking Strategies that are purely internal are no longer sufficient. Many news websites still use this old-fashioned approach.

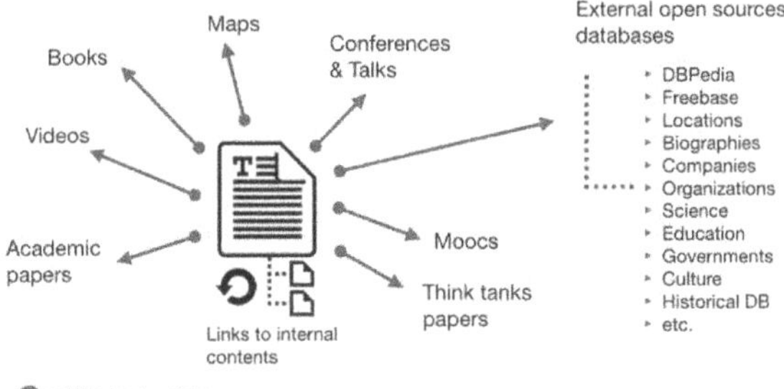

Fig. 7.2 - Linking strategies that provide greater context add deeper value to a story. Many modern technology websites and some news websites use this powerful way to surface stories.

What Can Businesses Learn from AP and the BBC?

There are valuable lessons here that can be applied to many business practices. The AP way can be replicated where products and services can be marked up using semantic markup that automates the surfacing and repurposing of the content through search, in direct response to relevant search queries.

This overcomes issues such as the need to focus on particular keywords with the production of 'thin' content or the need to have website pages specifically optimized for particular search queries and it allows a saving in costs that would have gone into the production and maintenance of those pages.

The BBC approach is perfect for any business that produces content and uses that content to be part of the online conversation. The curation of articles and the inclusion of social media sources and reactions in its overall presentation allows it to become a key component of the stories that are important to it.

Winning Strategies

Use structured data (if possible) on static web pages and on product pages so they can be repurposed, by search and mobile apps, in an automated way. AP partnered with financial firms that were already producing data in a structured way so it is worth here asking manufacturers of products whether they are already producing product descriptions in a structured data way.

Use a structured approach to curating and presenting unstructured content to help create clarity, context and relevance. Rationalize the various streams of content production so that they make sense for your target audience in terms of brand values and vision.

Link everything to the unique selling point (USP) of your business.

Use your strengths to decide the best way to tackle the issue of content creation, context and relevance.

Use content contextualization as a means to add value to what you do and avoid the commoditization trap.

Do not rely on internal linking strategies to surface content from your own site, link to authoritative news sources and articles that create a deeper picture for your online visitors.

Semantic Search Action List for Step #7

1. Create a list of subjects that covers the entirety of your content creation activities. You're looking here for classifications of some sort that are industry-specific to you.

2. Examine the list you have made with a critical eye and now cross out anything that is an overlap or is too tangential to really add value to your business website.

3. Match each of the values that best represent your brand identity with the most obvious classification that labels your content. For example, if you've chosen "fun" as a brand value it may be easiest to match it with "pictures", "memes" and "video" in your content creation than, say, "articles" or "white papers".

4. If possible, create menu items in your website navigation that closely describe the classification labels of your content.

5. If you cannot implement structured data on your website manually see if you can use any of the many ready modules created for the different types of CMS that exist. Test how search engines see it using Google's Structured Data tool: http://bit.ly/2P09bkv

6. Be familiar with the words and phrases that are commonly associated with your business. Use them appropriately in the content you create to highlight the focus of each item of content and help group items of content together.

7. Where possible, when cross-linking pages on your website use the terms you have listed in point six, above.

8. List websites that are authoritative in your industry or business type and determine how you can use them as reference to add greater value to the pages you create.

9. Always demystify terminology you use by linking to definitions that explain it.

10. Where possible use article-specific images to illustrate your content. Make sure they are: relevant, contextual and industry/business specific.

Step #8
Hashtags

 # Use hashtags to enhance your digital identity and add context to your content.

Hashtags (#) are a type of metadata tag used to categorize content that is shared across the web.

There are a lot of benefits to using hashtags:

- Hashtags are indexed by Google and do show up in search.
- They allow content you share to appear beyond your followers by extending its reach through its importance.
- They begin to label the corpus of your content and shared posts adding to a sense of what you do and what you are associated with. The hashtag #thesnipermind, for instance, on Google.com surfaces a lot of my content: http://bit.ly/32dDQAh or content I have been associated with promoting my book on decision making.
- Hashtags help you become an authority in the eyes of Google as well as those who use search.

They are also either grossly overused or underused. There seems to be precious little middle ground and there's a good reason for that. Those who would be served best by keeping them in mind, frequently forget to use them because they focus on the content they need to create and the engagement they need to generate.

On the other hand, those who have somewhat thin content are looking to tick every single SEO box they can and use them for everything they do. They are also the ones who, mostly, sometimes succumb to the temptation to game them a little by stretching the definition of the categorization a hashtag represents.

So, how should #hashtags be used if they are to work for you? Here are some suggestions:

- **Be original.** Create your own hashtag and use it to set your brand posts apart from anything else you may do.
- **Be organized.** Use hashtags (you can use more than one) to group the business content you share in a way that it makes sense. Suppose, for instance, that you sell used cars, posts that are hashtag marked as #tyres, #usedcarparts and #usedcaroffers help provide a degree of clarity on what you do by grouping together parts of the content you share even when that content is interspersed with a lot of personal stuff.
- **Be opportunistic.** A hashtag gives you the opportunity to get your content seen by associating it directly with a trending story. Twitter and Google+ have trending hashtags that mark a particular story of interest on any given day. Provided what you do is actually connected, in some way, to the trend (so you're

not spamming) this is a golden opportunity that should not be missed.

- **Be consistent.** Hashtags can become part of your digital identity, helping to define who you are by highlighting your domain expertise. It helps to have a clear idea of what that domain expertise is for you and indicate it, using an appropriate hashtag.
- **Be creative.** Hashtags frequently become rallying cries around which the digerati can congregate. In that regard it helps if you have a rallying cry that actually can be mentally unpacked by the audience so that they can feel empowered, actively participating and able to 'own' the concept behind the hashtag.
- **Be aware.** Use your hashtags, where possible, to broaden the appeal and reach of your content and tie your brand values to what's happening in the world. (Word of warning: do not abuse this. The approach is responsible for most social media disasters I see.)

Track Your Hashtags

Use Tagboard (http://goo.gl/2RiaTA) to track hashtags and see what other people are doing with your hashtags. It's a paid service but you can create one tagboard for free. Use hashtags.org (http://goo.gl/yyzbLx) to discover trending hashtags as well as global hashtags you can use.

Use Twitter's own search (http://goo.gl/cmzjU) to see trending hashtags and to also search out new ones, or discover how far yours have travelled, who has reshared them and what appeal they had.

Semantic Search Action List for Step #8

1. Make a list of all the hashtags that completely describe your product and services.

2. Now make a list of all the hashtags that describe your brand values. Compare the list you made in Action Point #1 and this one and see where the overlaps occur. This helps become part of your digital marketing strategy that drives brand values and establishes your identity.

3. Make sure you use hashtags when you promote your content.

4. If your CMS supports it get into the habit of using hashtags to create relevant hierarchies across your content.

5. Use Google search to map the reach of your hashtags.

6. Reinforce those who share content with your hashtags by re-sharing it across social media platforms.

7. Encourage the creation of original content that uses your hashtags.

8. If you run marketing campaigns *always* use an original hashtag to make them stand out.

9. Look at the way market leaders in your industry use hashtags and emulate them.

10. Keep in mind that while hashtags can run into two-three words like #thesnipermind, for instance, they acquire true value when they are a single word search engines can understand like: #marketing #communication or #ethics. Use a mix of both to help create uniqueness and value.

Step #9
Ontologies

 # In a semantic web arranging your content in a way that creates Ontologies provides for an easy win.

It is no accident that in the field of philosophy ontology is the study of reality, existence and coming into being. In the fields of information retrieval (semantic search) and computing, ontology is the naming of the types, interrelationships and properties of the entities that exist (in reality or conceptually) and which define a particular domain of knowledge or expertise.

Now that we got this rather difficult definition out of the way (and I have simplified it somewhat here) it's worth mentioning that the reason we need ontologies is to simplify complexity. Consider this for a moment: If the automotive industry did not have ontologies then when it's time to look for a car you'd need to sit down with a dealer and pull up a tome the size of a large suitcase and begin to wade your way through it looking for the one vehicle you want.

Instead you already know whether you want to go for an SUV, a sedan or a sports car. These are ontologies which simplify your choice and they are broken down into further ontologies which guide you in your choice, narrowing it down to the one (or maybe a handful) of choices that faithfully fulfill your criteria.

Now imagine that's how semantic search works, using ontologies to quickly narrow down options that have to appear in response to a search query. It uses the categorization to quickly drill down to the data and deliver the best possible answer from the information it holds in its index.

There are two things to remember here and they are both equally important. First, unless the information has been indexed by Google (and any other search engine) it will not appear in search. Second, anything you can do to help make the process of creating ontologies, easier, is a win for you.

The subtext here is that Google and every other search engine out there does not have to provide the best possible answer to a search query, just an answer that's good enough from the information stored in its index. The best website in the world, holding the best information ever, on a specific subject, is useless if it cannot be indexed and its content accessed by search engine bots as easily as possible. As a webmaster (or an entrepreneur working online today) it is *your* job to make sure this happens.

So the question now clearly is what should you do to make sure your website uses ontologies in a way that helps Google index it better and understand its content more easily? In an experiment on ontological alignment carried out at the Sharif University of Technology, Tehran, researchers showed how different ontologies can lead to the same thing:

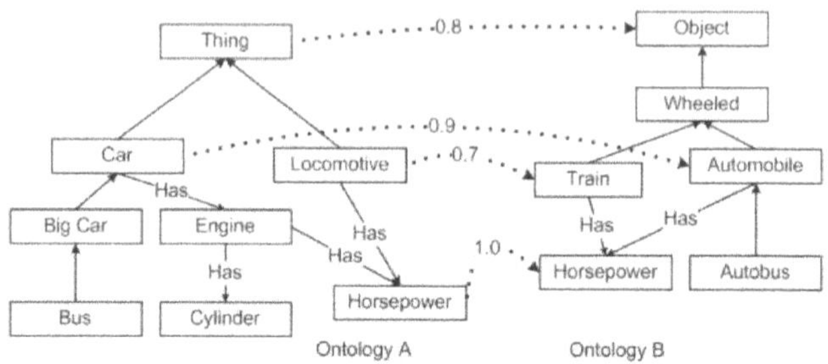

Fig. 9.1 - The values mapping the dotted lines show the exact correlation between entities in different ontologies.

So what should you be doing to help your site in this regard? There are several steps:

- **Group your content in a way that makes sense.** (if you look at the way articles I write are arranged on my website, for instance, anything that is practical and has to do with business appears under the "Observations" tab and anything that has to do with SEO and general web trends appears under the "Web View" tab, videos appear under "Video" and podcasts under "Web Talk". This helps Google better understand the context of the articles I write and determine the weighing it should give each in relation to my known expertise and authority on specific subjects.

- **Map your subjects.** The content on your website should map, in detail, the domain you are working in. If, for instance, you sell home insurance, house prices, home insurance, protection from natural disasters, case studies, scenarios, tips on saving money, unknown pitfalls and criteria for balancing the best house insurance on a budget, should be articles that you will need to have there.

- **Use your keywords.** Semantic search does not rely on keywords but that does not mean they're not important. Provided they crop up naturally and totally tie-in with what you're writing about, keywords and their naturally occurring derivatives and variations, help Google extract entities from the web page where they occur.

- **Link pages to additional resources.** Add extra value to each page, for your online visitors by adding to detailed resources on highly trusted websites (online newspapers, educational sites or Wikipedia, for example). There will always be other web pages with detailed, accurate, high-quality information related to what your business is about in the public domain. Avoid repeating information unnecessarily and link, instead to trusted resources. This helps to further increase the value of your page as a resource, since it groups together relevant, high-quality data.

- **Use Correct Alt text and Link descriptions.** In your page use correct, detailed Alt Text to describe the illustrations and images you use and do the same for any links leading to other parts of your site or other parts of the web.

- **Arrange your website navigation.** Make your website as flat as possible, arranging it so that its navigation closely reflects the ontologies you are trying to create.

- **Use #hashtags.** Where appropriate use hashtags to mark your content, particularly when you post your website content to social media platforms that accept hashtags (Twitter or LinkedIn). Search engines see that content, read the hashtags and then follow the link back to your website. The hashtags you use in your social media posts should accurately reflect the nature of the webpages you point to. A mismatch here will raise red flags that will put the trustworthiness of your website under a question mark.

As with everything else that has to do with semantic search the implementation of Ontologies requires careful thinking and a consistent, detailed, sustainable approach.

Consider that "Ontology" is strictly defined as an explicit formal specification of the terms in the domain and relations among them. The way you use hashtags to create groupings of content within your website (i.e. the domain) and the way you interlink pages (i.e. the relations amongst them) help better define, for search engines, the ontologies you're creating.

If it all sounds a little prescriptive it is because that is exactly what Ontology-building requires.

Semantic Search Action List for Step #9

1. You should include in your link descriptions and your Alt Text for images terms that are specific to the Ontologies you're creating on your website.

2. Audit content you have already created. Check to see if it contains the terms you need. If it is grouped under the right grouping. If it links to external, authoritative sources that increase the value of the page itself.

3. Formalize how you create your content by thinking about it as Concept > Attributes > Value. For example, if you're writing a review about a sports car you will need to think of its structure along these lines: Automobile > Fast Cars > Two seater. The strategy applies to any content and it creates a specifically identifiable value in how it will be indexed and then served in search.

4. Identify the specific technical terms you would use in each of the sections/segments of the content you create. Create a consistency guide that, in theory, would allow anyone in your organization create content that is of the same high-quality and consistency in terms and approach.

5. Create a consistently logical approach to the purpose of every item of content you create. For example: Pictures/memes show fun activities, have a minimum of two people and are predominantly group shots.

6. Communicate the formal definitions of style you've created for your content to your entire organization. Do this even if it's just you and your dog that's running the show. The formal articulation of the approach will pay dividends moving forward.

7. Identify and embed, in the written content you create, commonly used phrases and questions that have to do with your business. For example: "Where can I get vegan pizza?" for a vegan restaurant or "best car wash near me" for a car wash with the words "near me" in the content replaced by identifiable places or landmarks that help search understand the location.

8. List all the attributes commonly associated with your brand/business. Examples can be: Waterproof Nike Running Shoes or Brazil Coffee Production. Try to work some of them in the headings and subheadings used in the content you create.

9. List all the terms and concepts commonly associated with the attributes you listed in eight above. For instance: waterproof shoelaces that go with your "Waterproof Nike Running Shoes". Or, ceramic coffee-beans grinder best suited to "Brazil Coffee Production".

10. Provide a whole experience on each page of content. For example: link to different types of grind and what they each do for the flavor and taste of coffee if you talk about coffee grinders. Or all the different shoe lace types available for running shoes.

Step #10
Website Design

 # The quality of your website design is still critically important to your ranking in search, but now it's more complicated.

Quite a lot has changed in website design since the very first edition of *SEO Help* came out and a lot has changed since the last one which this one is updating. While, almost everything I said in the last edition of this book still holds out (and if you haven't checked it out I would advise you to) I've chosen to take a different route in this edition.

The reason is that web design in the artistic sense of the word is now secondary to content and other factors which place function, squarely above form.

I am glossing things over a lot, obviously, to give you a generalized bird's eye view. Mobile traffic represents almost half of the entire web traffic globally. Smaller screens and almost ubiquitous connectivity have changed the context of how search is used.

This has led to the obvious situation of website design being used to deliver conversions and further drive brand appeal, brand values and brand message.

How?

This is where it gets interesting. Consider that every business has its own language. Media companies have producers and writers, actors and grips, distribution networks, script doctors and video masters. Fruit shops sell fruit and vegetables, they understand what a cantaloupe is and how a Fuyu Persimmon can be peeled. They operate in a world of perishables bounded by fresh herbs and spices and their powder-form equivalents.

The point is that the language of each business is a code of what it does. That 'code' unites everyone within your business with its customers outside it, so we shall call it the communication matrix. All the things found within a fruit shop (or a media company) also have a separate, symbolic existence in the balance sheets and spreadsheets created by stockists, suppliers, managers, accountants and database analysts.

The way the real world maps to the digital expresses itself in the design and functionality of your company website.

The design of your website then is a data interface. It captures data you need and it imparts data your customers and audience need. Get it wrong and you will find yourself with few conversions and falling sales and, worse, owning data you cannot use because you've been tracking the wrong things.

Get it right and it becomes a sales funnel that brings you money, extends your reach and gives you a bigger and bigger audience.

Semantic Search Action List for Step #10

1. Check your website's loading speed. A heavy website is a website that fails its audience by taking too long to load on their devices. If you had a wish about your website design, in regard to its UX and the end-user experience, what would it be? What's stopping you from implementing it?

2. Make a list of all the data your website needs to deliver to its visitors. In the instance of the fruit shop, for example, this would be merchandise, product availability, opening hours, additional recommendations of food items, maybe recipes, and so on. There would also be the visuals, which range from the fruit shop logo to the individual fruit and vegetable items that are part of the merchandise range.

3. Make a list of all the data you expect your website to capture from its visitors.

4. Look at the two lists from points two and three above. Is there an overlap anywhere? Is it easy to match one with another? Can it be tweaked to make it easier to match?

5. Now alongside the two lists from point two and three above list all the parts of

your website that deliver/capture the data. Is there an overlap here?

6. Compare all the data you have coming into your business and going out of it and see if anything is missing. If you're confident everything is as it should be, create one more list alongside the three you already have with each point of your website showing the number of steps that must be taken in order for the necessary data to be captured or transmitted. For instance, if in order to get the answer to a particular question; your audience has to register and download a white paper which needs to be scanned in order to find the answer, you'd number this as having three steps.

7. From the answer you have given in step six, above, can you reduce the number of steps required to transmit and receive data so that your website is as frictionless as possible?

8. If you haven't listed them already identify the data points which transmit your brand values to your audience. How are they expressed in the overall design of your website?

9. Using the list you made in point eight, above, check to see if there is a consistency in your approach. For example, if you're a customer-centric company and it is hard to reach out to you

you're not living up to your professed values.

10. Carry out one final test. Print out your website's homepage. Now on that homepage label all the parts of your website's design that either deliver or capture data. Explain the benefits of having that particular data delivered to the online audience or captured from it.

Step #11

Images

 # Images are an integral part of your SEO because they play a key role in semantic search.

Google has been working for some time on Entity recognition technology to help it read the objects within pictures: http://goo.gl/hmJfa6, and then work out the context they depict: http://goo.gl/AdFZP5.

This means that there is an ever increasing opportunity to be super-clever with your marketing and make a picture work for you by adding additional content layers that will help with your marketing, branding and overall visibility on the web.

If the pictures you use, for instance, act almost like a visual shorthand of sorts, summarizing the text content you have in place, you are basically increasing the options you have of your website to come up in response to a search query. You also add extra layers of data density which help Google determine the quality of what you do, its context, its value and its trustworthiness.

In the age of search the classic saying of "a picture is worth a thousand words" has transmuted to the new truth: *a picture is worth a thousand clicks.*

For that to happen however you need to now do more than just blindly tick the mental box that says "illustration needed" in your content creation activities and marketing efforts. That makes things tricky. Not every picture is worth a thousand words and those that are may not be worth the thousand words you are looking for.

So now you need to think visually not just in pictures you want to put out there but also in pictures that mean something to your audience and help drive the online connection you need for your brand. Think how hard it now is: You need pictures that are part of a shared language of communication between who you are and what you want to do and the audience you're reaching out to.

To work for you in the age of the semantic web and semantic search every image you use needs to:

- Be eye-catching and thought-provoking
- Help promote your brand
- Reinforce your brand values and principles
- Kickstart an online conversation with your audience
- Summarize some of the content it illustrates
- Stand out from your competitors

- Be as unique and original as possible (and these two attributes are not always tautological)
- Be fully integrated in your overall marketing strategy
- Get you fresh audience
- Work equally well across different screen sizes and devices

Clearly, this is a lot for any single image to do. Some may indeed do so because elements like subject matter, inspiration and availability of photo opportunities or available images have come together. Others will fall short of the mark.

Regardless, your task is to make sure that each image you post online ticks as many of these requirements as possible.

Consider the fact that we live and work in an attention economy. For anything to work: branding, learning, task completion, even reading this short paragraph, we need our brain to pay attention and focus on the task at hand.

We only pay attention to things we consider to be important. In order for us to consider something important we need to appraise its value and allocate it a priority.

Now think that the images you use have to help your audience understand that what your brand and business sis important to them. Which then means they need to pay attention to its marketing messages.

Hopefully, when you consider it like this, you begin to realize the scope of the problem and the task you've got when it comes to choosing images. Even the most important business in the world cannot be considered so important that everything it does is worthy of our attention.

This is why businesses that are good at marketing also post content that falls into the domain of social conscience, fun, entertainment, comment and wonder. These are touch points between the business or brand and its audience which allow it to secure the constant attention of its audience.

Pick your images with care

I know it's difficult to always find original images or very high-quality ones. Here however you have absolutely no choice. To use a poor image to illustrate the writing on your website is worse than using no image at all.

So here's what you really need to do:

- **Use large, high-quality images**. Optimize them for fast loading. Thumbnails and 200 pixel wide images are a definite no-no.
- **Pick your images to attract eyeballs**. View your website like a glossy magazine page. The pictorial material you place

there needs to stop the eye long enough for the text to work on the mind.

- **Try to tell a story**. Your image should be more than just a great picture. It should be part of your website's narrative. It should tell a story as well as sum up the article it is illustrating.
- **Be original**. This one, I know, is hard. It is not easy to find original illustrations or pictures and it is even harder to make sure that they synch with your page content to create an outstanding whole. Yet this is what you need to work towards every time.
- **Be consistent**. Websites that post pictorial content willy-nilly are missing out on the opportunity provided by synchronized brand marketing. Strive to create a consistent look and feel to your website's pictorial content and that, in turn, as you dominate search will help you win both brand recognition and visitor loyalty.

To understand the power of image branding consider the case of Darebee.com. The health & fitness website single-handedly popularized the line-drawn fitness image as an online resource. As a result its unique appeal and branding has created a visual style that makes it instantly recognizable even when its logo is not immediately visible: http://bit.ly/38R2CIE.

Optimize Your Pictorial Content for Fast Indexing

Optimizing the pictures on your website for fast indexing and higher ranking in Google's image search requires that you consistently tick a few search engine optimization boxes each time:

- Optimize your images for fast loading using either Photoshop to create web-friendly images or use Google's available, free online image optimizer: http://bit.ly/2SNbhqc.
- Make sure every image you post is labeled properly. So instead of loading image D230971.jpg on our imaginary leather goods site, relabel it to High-Quality-Brown-Leather-Wallet.jpg. Make sure that you hyphenate each word so that Google can read it properly.
- Make sure every image on your website has meta tags (alt tag) that describe the image in detail.
- Make sure your alt tag text adds further value to the content you illustrate rather than blindly repeat a description that's in the text of your website. For example: "A high quality leather wallet creates the impression of refinement in a gent" is way better than just "brown leather wallet" which is echoed in the image file name anyway.

Semantic Search Action List for Step #11

1. Create a list with the type of images that are industry-specific for you. If it is difficult to create a differentiated visual look this way, think what you need to do in order to achieve it with the images you use.

2. Go through your website and optimize any images that have not yet been optimized that may make individual web pages slow to load on mobile devices.

3. Whenever possible try to be original by taking your own shots or drawing your own diagrams and charts.

4. Always share the images you use on image-sharing sites like Pinterest and micro-blogging platforms like Tumblr.

5. Try to use images that contain complete, recognizable entities. For example, a full, baked loaf of bread in a picture used to illustrate content about a bakery. An outside shot of a car that immediately identifies the make and model for an image used to illustrate content for a car dealership and so on.

6. Create a consistent theme with your images. A travel company, for instance, should use images that are consistent with the bulk of its holiday destinations. This

should include identifiable landmarks and settings that create a consistent pattern that reflects the company expertise (i.e. beaches, chateaus, ancient ruins in terms of destinations and couples' pictures or family ones if the company specializes in a particular demographic).

7. Create a consistent feel with your images. Again check out to see how Darebee.com does it: http://bit.ly/2SM6qp2. Even more importantly check out the classifications that Google has identified match the site's pictorial workouts.

8. If you have premises try to have your premises included in some of the images you use to illustrate your content. Where possible your business logo should be in the shot.

9. Use local landmarks in your pictures and images that illustrate the content of your website. For example illustrate content that contains "Perfect coffee shop for business meetings with a view of the London Tower Bridge" with a London Tower Bridge in the backdrop.

10. Aim to have one central focus in your pictures, each time, that reflects the core concept of the article you illustrate. If you're talking about making organic wine, for instance, you will need a picture of the wine-making machinery as opposed to the

vineyard. Where possible include your logo and copyright, especially if you're sharing original diagrams that explain some aspect of your text-driven content.

Step #12

Podcasts

 # The sound of the spoken word has the ability to travel further than a web page.

It is a bit ironic that in the age of the web, when content gets delivered whisper-quiet to our mobile devices via an app, the spoken word has seen a resurgence thanks to podcasts.

There are many reasons why you should think of including podcasts to your content not least of which is convenience for your audience.

Others include:

- Flexibility of content - podcasts allow you to present things in a way more suitable to the spoken format.

- The better building of a brand identity - it is easier for your audience to identify with your brand when they feel they know the sound of your voice.

- Reaching a different audience - finding an audience can be opportunistic as people reach for something to listen to when doing other things.

- Broadening the format of your content - different content is consumed differently depending on available time and the inclination of your audience.

- Shareability – under some circumstances a podcast can provide an easily shareable item of content.

- Presence – it adds to the impact of your brand and the quality of your SEO efforts when you are present in many different channels.

There is a real temptation here to think that podcasts are an easy way to generate content. Resist it. Easy, they might be, when compared to, let's say, penning a 1,500 word article but that does not make them an easy win.

Like every other item of content you generate and that includes shares of other people's content in social media channels, opinions and comments, podcasts have to add to who you are, what you do and why you do it. And they have to do so in a convincingly high-quality way.

Podcasts, even more than the written word, help personalize you to your audience so you must treat them with the seriousness they deserve and do most of the work concerning focus and aims, before you even start to record them.

The Technical Details

If you're ready to go down this path you will need a few things:

- A good quality headset (they can be picked up at a relatively low cost from Amazon or any electronic store). Go for a wired one, as opposed to wireless as they provide the best quality.
- A suitable audio recording program. One of the best free ones on the web is Audacity. It can be downloaded free of charge here: http://goo.gl/ARs0.

And that's it. Check out to see how I create mine: http://goo.gl/PQ6Asi. Notice I keep them short on purpose (that's by design). The length of time you make each podcast is entirely up to you. Consider however that it is always a combination of subject matter and audience type. Whatever you decide to do the key is to be consistent.

I use a professionally created intro and outro for my podcasts and I have a little bit of assistance after I record them in that I send the recording to the team that uploads it to the site. They edit everything down to the required length.

You do not need to do anything so fancy. What you do need to do however is remember that the spoken word is different to the written one. I usually write out my podcasts while travelling and then read them out aloud and change them for flow, clarity and euphonia (sentences that just sound good together).

I also keep the flow of ideas in a way that is easy to remember (which means I structure them differently to maintain clarity).

Finally, the Channels

Once you have your podcast you will need to think of how you can best make use of it. Obviously your website will be one venue. Podcasts can also be uploaded to YouTube and used with an image, a number of rotating images or additional text. YouTube provides a digital means to easily find and reshare (or even embed) your file. As the world's second largest search engine YouTube provides you with a way to be discovered plus a number of ways to have your content appear across the social web.

Soundcloud (http://goo.gl/xqLgL) is the equivalent of YouTube for soundfiles (admittedly before Google acquired YouTube). It allows you to upload your podcast there, it provides an additional point of independent discovery of your soundfiles and it is also easy to reshare across the social web (and that includes G+ where the soundfiles play like native YouTube files).

Some podcasters who have regular content find a good audience by submitting their podcast feed to iTunes and making it available for iPhone users. If you want to go down that path the instructions are here: https://apple.co/38K16YV.

Finally you may want to consider the possibility of using an app to allow Android users to subscribe and listen to your podcast. Android users can listen to iTune podcasts through a number of apps and creating an app specifically for your podcast may be expensive but if you do go down that path it will help with your branding plus you will have access to statistics that will help you better understand audience behavior.

Podcasts and Search

Having a podcast is not much use if it does not help you with greater visibility in search. Here's how this happens:

- Greater visibility in social media through shares and reshares of your podcasts leads to citations, brand awareness and even traffic directly to your website.

- The channels through with your podcasts are disseminated (YouTube, SoundCloud, iTunes, Spotify) should all point to your website and should all mention your brand. This helps with the entity-building part of semantic search.

- Your brand name should be clearly presented at every podcast.

Semantic Search Action List for Step #12

1. Make a list of the brand values and brand topics you will promote through your podcast. Draw lines between values and topics and then explain, briefly, how they are linked. Example: A tech firm that uses its podcast to promote transparency in its industry because it believes in equal access to information and values the individual.

2. Create a logical structure for your podcast: what will you talk about each time? How? Will you have guests? When? How will you treat them? Will you ask for a Q & A from your audience? How will you handle that?

3. Include the one "ask" that makes your podcast add value to your business: will you ask for subscription to your channel so you can build your follower base? Will you direct them to your "deal of the week"? It's up to you.

4. Have a good image that will be used to illustrate your podcast when you post it across social media channels. Take note that each has its own unique requirements.

5. Decide on the style of your podcast: funny? Serious? In-between? Will the 'voice' you use be chatty? Professional? To

make it sustainable it has to be something that comes natural to you.

6. Decide on the frequency of your podcast. Daily? Weekly? Monthly? – Why?

7. Get the best equipment you can for your podcast. Audio quality is important so get a decent microphone and get a pop filter or pop shield to help smooth uneven sounds out.

8. Create an online promotion strategy for your podcast that fits in with your brand's marketing strategy. Don't wait for it to be 'discovered'. Actively promote it like it's cost you thousands and thousands to produce and you need to get your money back.

9. Use your own website as the primary platform for your podcast. Integrated it fully in the content you offer.

10. Don't be afraid to experiment and re-adjust. Nothing is cast in stone. So keep a record of everything to refer back to. That shows you what works for you and what doesn't.

Step #13
Artificial Intelligence

 # Semantic search is intimately linked to artificial intelligence developments.

Let's get this straight: Artificial intelligence, despite massive breakthroughs, is not very smart and it is unlikely to be smart in the conventional, human sense of the word for a very, very long time.

This also means that we're safe from killer robots which should give us sufficient peace of mind to focus on the things that really matter, like engaging in top-notch quality search marketing activities.

Artificial intelligence is however an incredibly useful tool that makes search, faster, more accurate and more nuanced than ever before. It is in the last word that all the magic sauce of the role of artificial intelligence in search is contained.

To understand this consider that semantic search is all about relationships between entities (nodes and edges). Those relationships constantly change. They become stronger or weaker. New ones are forged.

The dynamic is hard to track using traditional means (i.e. search algorithms that work on the presumption of fixed values in the connection between entities). Artificial intelligence creates a considerable shortcut to this by establishing knowledge domains (i.e. websites that are already considered to be good at the information they provide on specific subjects) and then using its own analysis and understanding of their content to serve up results in response to search queries.

The bottom line: the deployment of artificial intelligence in search creates a fast-moving target for anyone who's still in the game of "chase the search engine" in order to rank well in search.

The good news? All of the action points in this book and virtually every single step in it are designed to give you the granularity you need in:

- your website content
- search engine optimization efforts
- and content creation strategy

The action points in each Action List, in their totality, help you move your SEO efforts in the right direction for visibility in search that lasts. This way you will never have to worry about chasing Google or any other search engine, nor will you have to worry about Google updates negatively impacting your website.

Semantic Search Action List for Step #13

1. What is your website's "Domain Knowledge"? What is it known for in your industry? If you haven't defined that (e.g. High-quality, low-mileage used cars or ancient grape seed organic wine,) then you will find it harder to increase your visibility in search. So, let's narrow it down.

2. Look at the Domain Knowledge label you have decided on. Now list the number of articles on your website and posts on your social media accounts that accurately fit into that label.

3. Your content creation efforts needn't necessarily be 100 per cent on your Domain Knowledge. You can be tangential and expand provided your content is mostly centered on your website expertise.

4. Look at the photographs and images you use to illustrate your content. Do they accurately depict at least some of your Domain Knowledge?

5. Look at your social media posts. Does the subject matter of articles and images you share on social media platforms fit in, at least partially, with your Domain Knowledge?

6. Look at your videos and podcasts (if you have some in place already). Do they accurately showcase your Domain Knowledge? Bear in mind that video and audio are semantically

dense media. They need to squarely fit into your Domain Knowledge to work for you.

7. Examine your hashtag strategy. Hashtags are covered in Step Eight of this book. If you haven't looked at that chapter yet now's the time to refresh your knowledge. Do they, mostly, depict your Domain Knowledge? If not, can they be tweaked to rectify that?

8. Make sure your website content answers questions your target audience has and it is not, mostly, about promoting your business and brand.

9. Make sure you've cross-linked your website with all your social media platform points of presence.

10. Artificial Intelligence in search means that everything now counts and the concept of semantic density which I mentioned in Step Two of this book becomes really important. Nothing can be considered too small or without consequence. Every SEO action you undertake, from alt tags to hashtags, link descriptions to link anchor text, counts.

Step #14
Presence

 # Creating authority and trust in your digital presence is more vital than ever.

What if I started this chapter with a detailed recipe for chocolate chip cookies? Everyone likes them. You have paid money for this book so you know I know what I am talking about when it comes to search and marketing and (if you bought my last book) decision making but chocolate chip cookies are not part of my expertise. At least as far as you know.

A Google search for my name next to chocolate chip cookies will reveal nothing to convince you to try my recipe. The normal reaction here is to ignore it completely and also wonder whether you've done the right thing buying this book and trusting in my advice to help your SEO efforts.

It is the same across the web. Your digital presence, the content you produce, the posts you reshare, the comments you make and the online conversations you engage in are part of your identity. They showcase your interests, thinking, expertise and authority and help those who come across them trust you for some very specific things.

In the previous edition of this book; this chapter was focused on Authorship. Virtually everything that I covered back then still stands, including the ten steps at the end of that chapter. By changing this to "Presence" in the current edition and adding ten brand-new actions steps I am expanding on the subject.

To return to the example of my chocolate chip cookie recipe which, as things stand, you'd be right to be reluctant to try let's consider what happens next. Suppose that despite the natural and entirely understandable reluctance to trust the culinary skills of a writer whose expertise is marketing, search and decision making, a small percentage of my readers were curious enough to give it a go; make the cookies and taste them.

Suppose, again, that my out of the blue recipe was so successful, the cookies were so easy to make and so amazing to taste that they couldn't help but rave about them to *their* online following. And, their online following, having also tried my amazing chocolate cookie recipe also raved about it to the point that across many social media streams the talk to of the day was my amazing chocolate cookie recipe.

The chances that a writer of mostly technical books would come up with such an amazing chocolate chip cookie recipe are so slim that journalists, food bloggers and even some chefs couldn't help but comment on it, seek out interviews with me on my amazing chocolate chip cookie recipe and quote me on how I came to put it together.

This is what will happen next as a result of all this: Any of you reluctant to try it in the first instance will now make haste and try it out and blog about it. The smartest amongst you will talk about your initial reluctance, making it part of the story, while the ones who are less confident will simply ape comments and analysis already out there. Your voice will add to the signal about my amazing chocolate chip cookies.

I, of course, will by then have started expanding my career and you would see me appear on food shows, guest-blog on successful restaurant websites and pen the odd article on how marketing skills and cooking are not really that much different as they both require using ingredients that are far from original to create a mix that makes you stand out from the crowd.

Hardly anyone would stop to think whether I should be trusted to create food recipes. Google search will more than probably serve my one page with the chocolate chip cookie recipe on my website that is filled to the gills with articles on marketing, web trends, search and marketing analyses, pretty high.

It will also recalibrate its value of me as a trusted chocolate chip cookie recipe source, which is the whole point of all this.

How? Why? Because everything we talk about in semantic search and by association everything we talk about in marketing and branding today are subject to the flow of data.

All the issues we have when it comes to succeeding in search, marketing and branding and, by association, having a sterling reputation and being seen as trustworthy, hinge on the correct or incorrect handling of the 4Vs of Volume, Velocity, Variety and Veracity that are the foundational pillars of data.

I talk about the 4Vs in Step #18 of this book so here I will only say that it doesn't matter if we are talking about Big Data in the traditional sense of massive amounts of information captured from a single or a handful of sources or Small Data captured in volume across many different sources. The challenge is the same.

The success of my presence, the success of the presence you want to create on the web hinges not just on volume (i.e. the amount of information and content you pump out) but also on citation velocity, citation variety and most influential citation (i.e. when other experts cite you as a source or talk about you favourably).

There are mathematical calculations behind all this that ascribe a specific algorithmically determined weight to your presence which makes it 'trusted' in the eyes of search engines and, as a result, visible to more people across the web.

Engagement, interaction and impact are metrics that should concern you about your digital presence. The Virgin Group of companies, for example, brings in more than $21 billion in revenue each year, yet Richard Branson, its founder, spends a lot of time each day developing, still, the power, perception and reach of his presence on the web.

As you can probably guess I can write an entire volume about this alone. This is not what this book is about however so let's get to the practical actions steps you need to keep in mind.

Semantic Search Action List for Step #14

1. To develop your presence on the web you need to be selective on your subject matter. Pick your range of activities or expertise. These are the things that you will mostly talk about. You may see Richard Branson (and even me in some cases) talk online about a great variety of things but the brand in both these cases is really the person. Branson has used his public persona to drive interest in his business ventures and I write about a variety of things I am passionate about. My intention is to make my audience realize that in each case I am equally genuine and focused on delivering something of real value to the reader. You may need to be a little more selective in order to get faster, deeper results.

2. Hone your style. Allow your personality to seep through. Don't hide behind facts and adopt a safe drone persona that simply recites what's out there. Be as real as you can be.

3. Show your humanity. You're not in business just to make money. There is something that drives you that is unique to you. Find ways to surface that passion.

4. Use every means of communication available to you. The web is about connection and interaction. Without reach and engagement you may as well produce beautiful content in a vacuum flask. So, use pictures, video, writing, comments and even memes to find and connect with your audience.

5. Be consistent. Your audience gets to trust you because it begins to understand you. Articulate your values to yourself (first) and then your audience through your content and actions.

6. Be real. Engage in conversations, share opinions and really listen and respond to your audience.

7. Invest the time. Despite everything being digital there are no viable one-to-many shortcuts of amplification that will give you the same results as a personal response to an online conversation.

8. Be intentional. Align your goals, values and principles with who you are and who you want to become. Identity curation is as important for a brand as it is for an individual.

9. Be good. It needs to be said now: strive to add positivity and deliver value to the world whether digital or not.

10. Evolve. Continue to develop and evolve in line with technology and the fluidity represented by the modern marketplace.

Step #15
Google Properties

 # The web is truly global but it works best at being truly local.

The introduction to this chapter is something I first mentioned at a presentation back in 2007. At the time it sounded more aspirational than true. Today it is the way the web works.

The contents of a website get indexed so they can be used to answer search queries. Transactional search queries may still be just twenty per cent of the total number of search queries Google serves each month but it is this twenty per cent that puts money in your pocket.

Transactional search queries usually have answers that are relevant and local. If you want to take advantage of this you need to take advantage of some of the Google properties that allow your website to show up on local searches.

These include:

- Google Maps (https://www.google.com/maps)

- Google My Business (https://www.google.com/business)

Google has an online tool to help guide you through the choice of options that's right for your business: https://smallbusiness.withgoogle.com Even if you're an advanced user it helps to go through the process and explore all the options as it may give you an idea or two.

"Google Maps" and "Google My Business" allow you to create a digital presence and be found online even if you don't have a website. They also allow you to upload pictures, garner reviews, engage with your online audience and create exactly the kind of digital presence we talked about in Step #14 of this book.

It's an easy win with zero costs beyond your time and effort and you should take advantage of it. As a matter of fact an unwritten rule of the AI-driven semantic search universe is that you should take advantage of every opportunity you can to promote your website, boost your digital presence and add to the semantic density of your digital identity.

Semantic Search Action List for Step #15

1. Claim every Google property you can.

2. Be consistent in how you describe your business in each one.

3. Put in details like website, contact email and phone numbers and practical

information such as opening and closing hours (if pertinent).

4. Add good quality photographs of your place of business and your team.

5. Respond to reviews good and bad, fairly and promptly.

6. Integrate your digital and physical presence so that they are actually one instead of two distinct ones that are only linked by your business address and phone number.

7. Repurpose existing content material by changing its format for different channels.

8. Make sure #hashtags match across all your social media channels and profiles.

9. Cross-link everything so that those who find you on one digital property can find you in others.

10. Actively ask for honest reviews from those you do business with.

Step #16
Video Marketing

 # Video marketing, done right, is the only shortcut you have to building trust on the web.

There are four 'easy' steps to building trust in any relationship and they are:

- Contact
- Perception
- Assessment
- Connection

The formula is the same whether we are talking about an online or offline environment. Online it becomes commensurably harder because there is no corporeal presence, it takes time to collect all the communication signals that body language usually conveys. It is easy to misinterpret a message.

Video marketing is not new. It's been around as long as there has been a commercial online world. In the early days of the web, video was seen as the digital equivalent of the TV commercial. It became another means to market from one-to-many at an ever decreasing cost.

On April 23 2005 Jawed Karim, one of YouTube's founders posted the first video on the site called "Me At The Zoo" (http://goo.gl/gQVsB) documenting a few moments of his trip to the San Diego zoo and sparking off, in the process, the viral video marketing trend we experience today.

It is true that video can do all of the following:

- Allow you to project, unambiguously, the impression you want to project.

- Enable you to leverage YouTube's presence and traffic on the Web and find an audience you did not even know existed.

- Integrate the video into your ongoing marketing and out-reach campaign.

- Generate buzz in social media networks.

- Become part of your search marketing, helping to inform who you are, as a business, and what you do; in Google's semantic search index.

- Increase consumer engagement with your brand by helping the audience attain a better understanding of you as a person.

All of these activities also contribute to the building of trust necessary for people you don't know to want to do business with you.

Trust is hard enough to generate offline, where physical access answers most of the fundamental questions we have about a person or a business; on the Web, the task becomes that much harder. The mechanism that generates it is more difficult to set up. Yet that doesn't mean there is no trust-generating mechanism and there are no steps that can be taken to create it.

To better understand how trust is generated, and its benefits, consider a study commissioned by Bazaar Voice, a global marketing agency with offices in New York, London, and Paris. This study showed that millennials, the generation of people born between 1977 and 1995, will number more than 1.6 billion. By 2020 they will have more spending power than any other generation in history. At the same time, they have become the most resistant generation to traditional means of marketing, ever:

"This generation (sometimes referred to as Generation Y) has come of age being advertised to more than any generation in history. Baby Boomers may have seen magazine ads or billboards—Millennials see those, plus non-stop ads on their smart phones and Facebook.

"Their reliance on social disrupts all areas of business. They're connected and endlessly curious about what others are doing—and it flows right into how they shop. Like most generations, they trust opinions from consumers more than what brands say about themselves. Early social media adopters, they often understand social

better than the brands trying to reach them. So Millennials make their own rules of commerce."

In their report, tellingly titled *Talking to Strangers: Millennials Trust People Over Brands* , the analysts at Bazaar Voice pointed out that without consumer input and some form of direct contact, millennials "don't buy—almost anything."

The point of the report, which helps bring video marketing into full focus, is that the ingredient millennials look for in their behavior is trust. In fact, the sentence from the report just quoted could easily be rephrased to "without trust millennials don't buy—almost anything" without changing any aspect of its impact.

So how do you achieve this trust that has become the critical business challenge in the twenty-first century? How do you solve it so convincingly that it begins to create the necessary brand equity you want and bring in sales? Before I even answer that question, it's worth pointing out that although I use the term "brand equity" here because it is a commonly understood concept that creates a common frame of reference to build from, essentially the "equity" that is stored in any brand is the perception consumers have of its core values which then go on to inform their purchasing decisions.

Equity, in other words, can easily be replaced by that "magic" word again: trust. It goes without saying that brands that consumers trust have high equity value and vice versa. Video marketing helps a lot in this regard because it can help immensely with engagement.

Video Marketing and the Engagement Factor

When it comes to generating trust in video marketing, we frequently take into account factors such as appearance, setup, form, style, expertise, knowledge, and subject matter, which are all important elements. But none of these will work quite the way you expect them to if there is an ingredient missing from the equation. That ingredient is engagement.

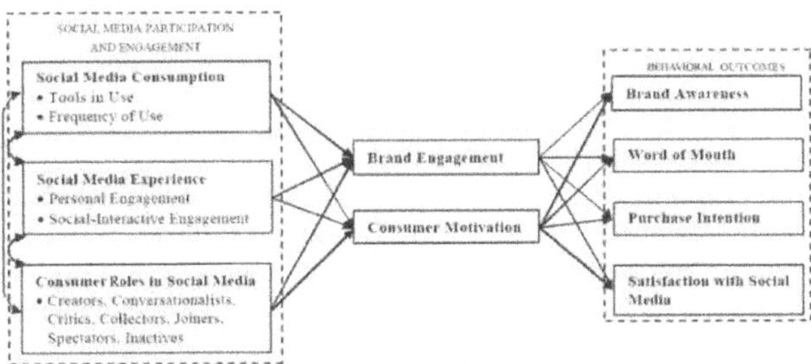

Fig. 16.1 - As the figure shows, engagement in a social media environment is key to transforming contact and interaction to deliver an outcome that will benefit your company or brand.

This is the ultimate channel for the kind of relationship management that marketing researcher Patrick E.

Murphy was envisioning when he wrote in a paper for the University of Notre Dame in Indiana: "[I] envision relationship marketing as passing through three stages: establishment, maintenance and reinforcement." The name of the paper was *An Ethical Basis for Relationship Marketing: A Virtue Ethics Perspective.*

Video marketing provides an unparalleled opportunity to establish a channel that helps initiate all three stages of relationship marketing. The reason it can become so effective lies in the disambiguation of intent that the direct contact with another person whose body language you can see and whose eyes can meet brings into the medium of communication marketing.

Suddenly, it is not just what you say but how you say it and to whom that makes all the difference. This takes "marketing"—an activity that in the past was associated with mass media and mass communication and "one size fits all" approaches—and makes it personal, personable, and human.

Framing the argument in an article in London's premier marketing magazine, *The Hub* , Jason Sorley, shopper-marketing Director of Marketing Drive, wrote: "Only three percent of in-store marketing communications is currently passed and seen by shoppers, according to POPAI's MARI project, conducted by Sheridan Global Consulting. So, the biggest barrier facing a brand's point-of-sale is simply to get noticed. To look at the problem another way, consider that 97 percent of in-store communication is completely missed by shoppers." And he concluded that "brands that empathize both rationally and visually get more attention at the shelf."

We see here in this description a sudden alignment of aims. The ability to get noticed, which is what every company or brand wants, coincides with the ability to connect. And after a connection is made, after a brand is "talking" to its target audience, things change.

Marketing is then perceived differently by the consumer and it is assessed in a different light. Purchasing decisions are made based on shared values and personalized messages.

More importantly, the consumer feels that somehow they 'know' the brand because in their minds' eye they can now link it to the face they've seen and voice they've heard on the screen.

One final point here. We say "Video Marketing" but we don't mean TV-Ad style marketing. Video marketing uses the medium of the video to humanize the brand. And this is something you need to think a little about so it is clear in your head that what you're doing is using video to connect with your audience, not talk down to them. This is where YouTube really comes into its element.

YouTube Unpacked

When it comes to branding and marketing YouTube is both underused and misunderstood. The reason many businesses fail to grasp its value lies in the perception that it's a video-sharing site. It is, of course, but it is also so much more than just that.

Let's take a look: A video-sharing site usually is a vertical silo which acts as a platform for the dissemination of videos, usually through its own site and social media platforms. YouTube does that but that's where all similarities end.

With over 300 hours of video uploaded to YouTube every minute of the day the site holds depth (in terms of content) and breadth (in terms of content creator and visitor numbers) to completely transform its reach and power.

In addition to its size and popularity YouTube has a number of other features that make it unique:

- Comments made on YouTube videos can become part of brand engagement.
- The embedding of YouTube videos on other websites holds the potential to start the online conversation anew, with a new audience.
- YouTube videos feature high in Google search for relevant search queries.
- YouTube itself has a powerful, contextual search engine.
- YouTube has a predictive viewing function that is purely semantic in nature. It analyzes the viewing habits and viewing patterns of each personal profile and suggests videos most likely to fit into it, thereby making sure that people actually find new videos that are most likely to appeal to them.

- Videos saved to playlist by viewers become part of the online co-creational culture that helps find fresh audiences.

One of the reasons YouTube videos are such powerful brand marketing aids in a semantic web is because the visual element of a video makes it easy to absorb content on the fly and engage in a way that allows brand sentiment to surface.

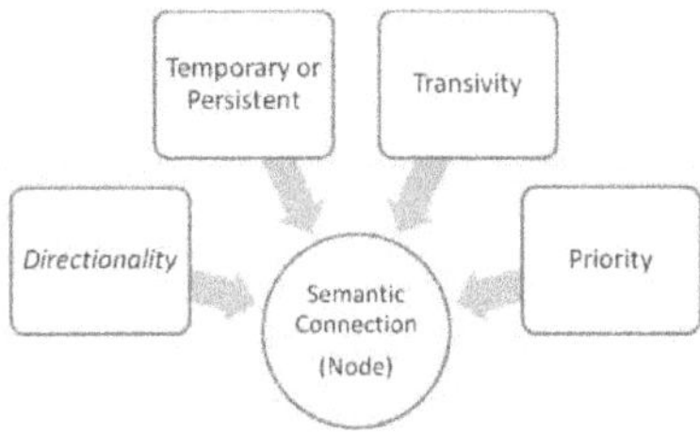

Fig. 16.2 - A connection made via a comment on a video (or a post) is weighed depending on who made it using four distinct attributes.

Videos make engagement easier which means they also make it easier to comment. When it comes to identifying how much weight to place on a comment made Google uses a number of criteria:

Directionality - where did the connection come from? Was the vicinity domain relevant (i.e. did the comment come from a group of people who regularly comment on this subject?) Was it from a bad neighborhood (which might have been trollish) or from a domain not usually associated with the current interaction?

Temporary or Persistent - was the connection haphazard, or by design? Did it lead to a real connection because it contributed something significant or was it a miss?

Transivity - does the current connection stand alone or are there shared friends and interests linking the commenter and the person who posted the video? If yes, what level are they at?

Priority - Was the connection one that resulted in a response and further engagement? Or was it ignored as irrelevant?

All this shows that comments and engagement, interaction and connections in the semantic web matter as much as they do in real life.

Creating YouTube Content

There are many different ways to create YouTube content. There are only two things to remember as you do this:

- Transparency demands content.
- Connection with the audience demands quality.

Both of these are synergistic. I will add the soft admonition that quality does not mean you should use a slick, high-powered production. Authenticity always trumps slickness and excessive packaging.

Transparency and connection are important for trust building. In the age of the semantic web they are key elements of your branding, audience-building and business-finding. They require that you start off with the human side of you first, before you start thinking about adding anything else to the mix.

Posting pictures of your staff, creating a video of your colleagues at work, video-documenting the making of a project, all of these are elements which create transparency. Add passion and drive into them and they also begin to acquire quality.

They are the steps which, by degrees, help humanize a business. In my consulting work I have come across multi-billion dollar businesses whose websites did not include a single picture of a person. The companies might as well have been staffed by cybernetic organisms from the Andromeda galaxy. A notion that was further reinforced by the corporate-speak in the content of their websites that could have easily been produced by soulless machines.

Here's a truth: Anyone can write about "offering a customer-centric service, pro-active service response to market conditions, online marketing outreach platforms and co-creational reinforcement of individual marketing initiatives leveraging tangential online networks." These are all terms culled from the websites of some of the largest companies on the planet.

None of these are good at generating warmth, empathy or humanity. If anything, their online content reinforces the idea that they are there to trick us into buying something we don't want, pillage the planet for profit and look out for themselves first, putting our own interests last.

A video presence cuts through all the nonsense. You can see, straightaway whether the person on the screen is sincere or not. You can decide whether they are as passionate, driven and humanly fallible as any of us or, if they have been trained to treat people with disdain and use company power as a shield to hide behind.

I could detail here all the psychological and emotional trigger points that a visual presence sets off but the point of this book is to be quick and actionable and already, in these later chapters, I have taken some liberties with length. So it is sufficient to say that you know in your gut when something is right (and there *is* a scientific explanation for that phrase and reaction, now). You intuitively know when things are "right" or "wrong" and even if you're not 100% sure in a first contact scenario, the moment you see a follow up video, you can verify your instincts.

Creating YouTube content becomes easier when you start to look at all the areas of operation of your business and then think of just how you could invite your target audience in there, to see them:

- How business is done

- Who does it

- How content is created
- How you treat each other within your business
- What your values are, internally

All of these are aspects of your business that drive sentiment and identity. Finding ways to project them without being preachy or turning the opportunity into plain advertising is always a challenge. It requires a certain degree of empathy and a willingness to be open and vulnerable (in other words human). Tackling it, kick-starts the process that bridges what a business does with the people it hopes to do business with.

In creating content for YouTube remember a few basic rules:

- Authenticity trumps packaged videos
- Engage and respond to comments on videos
- Try to turn each video into a real two-way conversation rather than just broadcasting
- Branding should always be secondary rather than key in your video content
- Value for the end-user should always come first
- Videos, like written content, should answer possible questions your potential customers have in mind

- Your description and video titles on YouTube should accurately reflect the content of your video

- The YouTube Channels you set up (and you can have more than one) should be as closely reflective of your website content categories as possible

In creating your YouTube content you still need to think like a filmmaker in the sense that there has to be a narrative structure and rhythm to each video and then all your video marketing in general.

To best help you understand how this can work check out one of the articles I wrote on the subject: http://goo.gl/wd5COf. The rule of thumb is that you need to be able to look at your finished video critically and ask: does it capture your attention long enough to want to make you engage further with the brand and the company behind it? If the answer is no then you may need to revisit the video a little and make sure it becomes more compelling.

Semantic Search Action List for Step #16

1. Make sure that you have a YouTube account to begin with as, without it a big slice of the audience you seek to connect with with your video marketing will be beyond your reach.

2. Have your YouTube account linked to your website.

3. List all the topics, relevant to your business which you think your audience would love to learn about in a more visual medium.

4. If possible, have a guest or two allowing an interaction to take place. This always generates a more interesting, natural format.

5. Think about your logo (if you are going to use one) and a consistent brand message that will stand as a kind of shorthand of your brand's identity.

6. You need very little to get started with video marketing. A reasonable quality web camera, a headset and microphone and as good lighting as you can possibly manage. Provided you have that with as few distractions in the background as possible you're good to go.

7. Integrate video in your website text content, reinforcing what you write with rich media.

8. Make full use of YouTube's optimization tools by having a complete and accurate description of your video.

9. Make full use of YouTube's analytics to track the appeal of your video.

10. Don't forget to share your video content as video content across different social media networks.

Step #17
Searcher Intent

 # Understanding searcher intent is key to getting to the point where the user-experience is overwhelmingly positive.

What every business owner, startup entrepreneur, webmaster and shopkeeper in the world would love to know the most is what do their customers want.

If they knew that they'd be able to satisfy their need, for some reasonable compensation of course, and this book and countless other business books like it would never need to be written.

Using analytical tools and creating a pathway designed to capture the necessary data a smart marketer today would know:

- Where the potential customer landed
- How long he stayed there
- What he did next

Multiply that by, say, a modest factor of just 1,000 data points and suddenly you begin to get a very clear picture of customer behavior that not only shows intent but also habits, perceived value (of your product) and general journey.

To use a very crude example suppose I saw that those who look at my book, *The Sniper Mind* on Amazon; in their majority, go on to check out golf, baseball, and basketball gear (which are mentioned as cognitive activities in the book), my content to promote the book would then have to move away from say "cognitive research" articles and focus more on competitive sports.

I would have to examine and mention the decision-making process involved in activities such as playing baseball, basketball or golf and analyze the direct benefits players would get from reading my book.

My advertising (if I actively engaged in any) would then also have to change to reflect my deeper understanding of my audience's interests. This would change the context in which my ads would appear on the web and in search. My targeting of influencers and podcasters would also change to reflect the concerns and needs of my coffee-guzzling, golf-playing demographic. My social media stream would also undergo a change of flavor.

You can see how it's all linked.

Google has released a mountain of data showing that A. The traditional marketing funnel is now as dead as the Dodo (primarily because every time people use their devices to carry out a search they reshape the funnel according to their needs and their place in the customer journey) and B. Search behavior is driven by emotional states so that the exact same search terms used at different times and different locations and, even, different devices indicated different searcher intent.

As Google put it: "...the six canonical needs of Kantar's NeedScope: "surprise me," "help me," "reassure me," "educate me," "impress me," and "thrill me,"" are behind the motivation of searchers to do something in each particular case and what they do depends upon their emotional state, not the search term they have used.

Google identifies as many as 2,000 touchpoints in some customer journeys and says that in order to take advantage of correctly having understood searcher intent websites must then:

- Provide local inventory information so they can see what's in stock nearby.
- Develop how-to videos.
- Offer the ability for consumers to seamlessly check out with an "instant buy" button.

Searching Beyond Purchase

Another point made by extensive Google research is that there are many customer journeys that do not end the moment a purchase has been made.

For example, the purchase of a flight and a holiday continues with searches about luggage, passport holders, tourist attractions and even airport-to-hotel connections and local food menus.

The purchase of a flat screen TV is followed up by searches on how to fine-tune it, care for it and what accessories can be linked to it.

All of this is material that now needs to be taken into account and suitable content has to be produced to deliver a satisfactory level of user experience.

The degree of satisfaction that online visitors feel when they come across your content is a key element that drives brand appeal and brand value. Brand appeal leads to repeat business and a willingness to engage with the brand message across social media platforms, while the perception of brand value delivers increased market share.

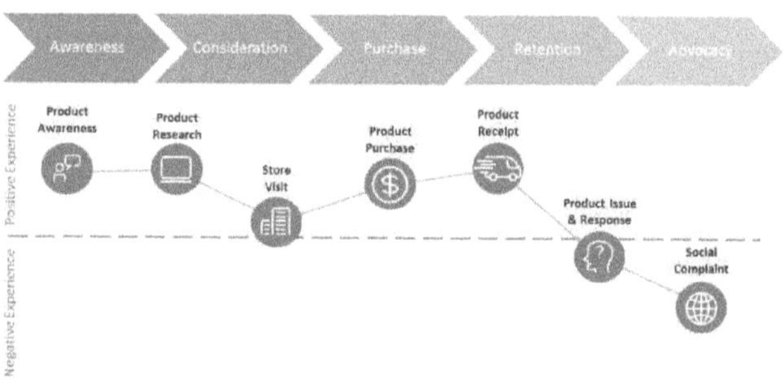

Fig. 17.1 – The customer journey trajectory has significantly changed over the last ten years.

To better understand the impact of searcher intent consider that marketing that is still using the approach of the past that employed demographics would, logically, target young couples and new parents with baby product adverts. Yet, market research and online surveys reveal that up to 40% of baby product purchases are made in households that have no children.

The message is clear: traditional marketing approaches, just like traditional SEO techniques no longer deliver the expected outcomes. Broader thinking is required. An approach that takes into account human behavior and actions which are used to divine intent.

The thing to remember about marketing, branding and search, in this environment, is that it goes beyond traditional demographics to reach a connected audience that has overlapping needs and wants that cannot always be easily ascertained beforehand.

This makes the customer journey extend beyond its purchase point. Paradoxically the quality of the user experience and the true long-term value of the customer journey are both defined by what happens after purchase has been made and the relational exchange of money for goods or services has transpired. Brands and businesses that do badly here are still caught up in the past.

Semantic Search Action List for Step #17

1. List all the different ways you track the behavior of your online visitors. Next to

each analytics channel you use list what you believe its data shows you about your online visitors and explain how you verify that.

2. List all the different situations you believe would lead a person to visit your website with the intent of doing business with you.

3. List who is your target audience. Now list all the instances where someone may come to do business with you without being in your target audience. What do you think motivates that person to enter into a transaction with you?

4. Intent leads to action. List what you believe those who come to your website started off with, as an initial intent. Map where do you think they would start off with in order to get to your website.

5. Now match what you've created in step four above with the subjects you usually create content about. Is there anything you missed? Are there overlaps that create duplicate content or content of poor value? Either fill in the gap by adding that subject matter to your list or merge two subjects to create stronger content.

6. List two areas of expertise in your business that could be predicted by studying consumer behavior. For instance, someone booking flights is likely to also

need accommodation. Depending on where they look for that accommodation and its time span you can predict if it's a business trip or a holiday.

7. Create a content plan that addresses the predictive area of expertise you worked out in point six above.

8. Make a list of all the consumer or online visitor behaviors you could use as a signal to make an informed prediction about intent.

9. Associate each of the behaviors you listed in point eight above with a hashtag or some keywords or some subject matter specific to your business or industry.

10. Check to see how many of the behaviors you listed in point eight above are represented or reflected in the content you create on your website.

Step #18

The 4Vs

 # When everything is data, data is everything.

The semantic scholar website at semanticscholar.org is "a project developed at the Allen Institute for Artificial Intelligence. Publicly released in November 2015, it is designed to be an AI-backed search engine for scientific journal articles."

The website uses groundbreaking AI and engineering to understand the semantics of scientific literature to help Scholars discover relevant research. To do this it needs to understand the value of each scientific paper and, even more crucially, its relevance.

The semantic scholar website is narrow and deep in concept and scope. Yet within the boundaries of scientific research there exists the potential for search queries to find the wrong results (or none at all). Its AI engine doesn't just need to understand what each scientific paper uploaded is about; it also needs to understand its importance in relation to its subject matter.

To do this it uses three key metrics: Citation Velocity, Citation Acceleration, and Most Influential Citations.

This way it gauges influence which then allows it to make an algorithmic pass at gauging importance.

The semantic scholar website is a very obvious example. The fact is that when it comes to algorithmically calculating influence, relevance and importance there are literally only a finite number of ways that the math can work.

To understand how far-reaching the 4Vs are check out Step #14 of this book (if you haven't already) and consider just how the algorithmically calculated value your digital presence is determined by the individual and then semantic values of the 4Vs.

In the last edition of this book I had to argue hard with my editor to include this chapter and the next one on the basis that though they weren't practical they provided knowledge that I thought was critical.

To show how far we've come consider that no one argued on including two chapters on data and real-world object representation.

Understanding the Flow of Data

Everything we do on the web is data. A comment made, a picture shared, a meme created, content you have slaved over for weeks and a video that took you a few minutes to shoot on a smartphone. All of this is data.

Data has an impact and that impact is governed by the 4Vs: Volume, Velocity, Variety and Veracity. These four attributes, taken individually and together help define the importance of a piece of information which is to say that they basically become the identifiers that allow us to filter important data from not-so-important data.

Across the web this distinction is important because it is used by semantic search as a first-layer of filtering to ascertain what is happening. It is this first-layer that I want to focus on right now because it is this that will guide most of your metrics when it comes to that moment when you will have to measure the effectiveness of your marketing efforts.

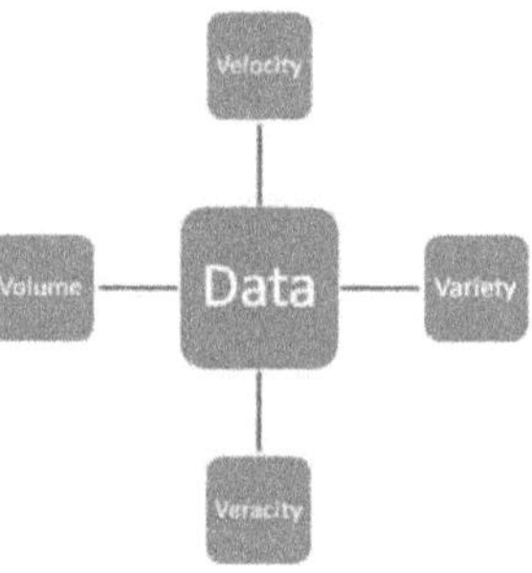

Fig. 18.1 - What happens to a piece of data on the web depends, largely, upon how far it travels and who then interacts with it.

The 4Vs that define all data, constitute a signal that means something about the data that you are sharing. How much data is being created (Volume), how fast it gets to travel (Velocity), who interacts, blogs about it, reshares it in a different context (Variety) and how trustworthy is everyone who's involved (Veracity) are what actually defines the intrinsic value of the data that you share.

To put this in a simpler perspective, the greatest idea in the world, shared in the woods with some bears is unlikely to have any impact on the world or do anything to enhance your reputation (unless, perhaps bears start using smartphones and social media).

You probably know from your own interaction with content that all of these things play a role when you decide what to read and what to reshare. How we evaluate content does not rely just on the perceived quality of it. Like everyone else we're also swayed by its perceived popularity or importance that is suggested by the way others interact with it and talk about it.

While we'd like to think that we judge all content on its merit and read everything carefully the truth is that when we are faced with so much content that we cannot, realistically, assess it all, we use the same shortcuts in our assessment as everyone else.

We employ a complex network of relationships to sift through content for us and we engage with some of it based solely on our perception of the importance our network has given it.

This should also be your cue for realizing two very important things: First that the quality of the content you produce is a relative metric that depends upon its relevance to your audience and second that content that fails to resonate is unlikely to do very well, despite it being useful. This 'resonance' with an audience is hard to describe but in broad strokes it requires a certain degree of humanity and empathy. The content has to touch upon some aspect of humanity, however small that might be. You have to feel a little of the issues your audience is grappling with.

So, a long list of questions and answers that comprehensively cover a subject might be thorough and it might check the box marked "quality content" but it may also sound too impersonal and soulless to really connect with an online audience that has learnt to scan copy in order to evaluate it first and really looks for some hook to capture their attention.

The point of a book like this, of course, is to give you answers and quick actionables rather than tell you how hard it is to get content to appeal so here's the ultimate tip on that score:

Be You

That's it. Everything we have covered to date on each chapter and on the chapters that are coming up, really, show one thing only: You have to be unique. And unique requires you to be real. And real requires that you actually put out there who you are, what drives you, what you really believe in as well as what you're trying to achieve by way of business.

In the past we equated uniqueness with outlandish behavior, over-the-top exploits and larger-than-life personas. That was the world of last century that manufactured celebrities and used a one-way broadcast model to carefully feed us their personality. This is not the world we inhabit today. Uniqueness, today, is a careful synthesis of who you are and what you do, how you do it and how you communicate all of which is assessed in terms of its impact on the outside world: those you come in contact with.

How exactly you manage to do that in a way that helps you every time you market and every time you connect in the digital domain is up to you to solve. But solve it you must if you really want to succeed.

Your Digital Identity

The moment you step out of your house you're sending off signals to the world around you. The way you're dressed, how you carry yourself, the way you speak, the way you look around, how your hair is arranged, these are all signals that mark your identity, feed into conceptions you want to create and dissuade the ones you don't from forming in the first place.

In the physical domain none of us have any real choice. We exist within it in corporeal form whether we want to or not and we have had a lifetime to practice how we create the uniqueness of us. What really marks us in that domain is an incredible layer of data density. We leave our footprint, by way of activities and behavior that cement our reputation, wherever we go. From the moment we leave our homes to go to work, to the moment we go out shopping and socializing, we create a trail of our character, skills, beliefs and values that informs, in the minds of those we come into contact with, a solid sense of who we are.

More than that, it goes into creating our reputation. Depending on the impact of our personality and the extent of our circle of friends and acquaintances, others get to hear about us even if we do not directly come into contact with them. This kind of data density is critical if we are ever to get anywhere in the real world. Now when you compare this kind of data density to what we manage to achieve online with our occasional social media shares, occasional online interactions and occasional online posts you, hopefully, begin to realize why our online identity creation efforts are usually so woefully inadequate.

Everything we discuss throughout this book seeks to help you achieve as much of a data density in your online presence as possible. This way not only are you finding new ways to build connections and relationships with your online audience but you also begin to create the kind of digital identity that becomes your brand in a way that actually has substantial meaning for those who choose to engage with you and become *your* audience.

There is an understandable creep factor to the entire identity question. Not only do we, today, look at how we can quantify both identity and trust, breaking them down into their constituent parts and looking at how they can be replicated through action but we also talk about consciously fashioning both.

This brings into question the concept of authenticity. If our every online move is aimed at generating identity and trust just how authentic and spontaneous are we really? In truth you can fake being someone or something you are not, online, just as well as you can offline. In the short term it appears to be easy, but as the data about you accumulates the small white lies and the inconsistencies begin to build up until the entire edifice you have built begins to collapse under their weight.

The inability to fake anything in the semantic web for too long and the need to be there for the long term in order to make any decent amount of money (or achieve a decent digital identity) is what's behind the need for honesty being felt by business.

As data increases more and more technologies are springing up that allow us to make sense of it right at the point of collection. This requires on-board processing both of apps and software applications which are beginning to become more and more intelligent. The Internet of Things (IoT) where devices talk to each other is part of this, as indeed is the trend for wearable computing and cloud computing. All of these are basically iterations of the semantic search's concept of the transition from "strings to "things" and from "websites to people".

Basically, all of this is about people which means it is all about identity and relationships.

Over the next decade search will change beyond recognition. Cognitive computing will take off in a big way and robotics will change the way we do everything (again). What will not change in all this is you. Me. Us. People. Basically it is all about people doing business with people, interacting with people and meeting other people. It is ironic that it has taken the digital revolution which puts so much emphasis on robotics and artificial intelligence, to make people draw together, rediscover the value of meeting and working with other people and begin to prize being authentic and real (human in other words) first, before they can start to market and sell.

If you really want to future-proof your marketing and online branding there can be no better advice I can give you beyond striving, at every phase, to find ways to be more transparent, real and inclusive.

To do this you will need to constantly be alert to fresh opportunities to do so, be brave enough to attempt new things (even if it means having to put up with the occasional public failure) and be willing to experiment and push against the boundaries of what's possible on the web.

You will also have to strive to find ways to bridge the online/offline divide, creating a seamless whole from your business (if you work in both the physical and digital realm). If you happen to have on online-only business you are in a better position as 100% of your available time will be spent in this realm, which should provide you with the opportunities you need to create the granular, digital presence you need.

The 4Vs of Big Data (and semantic search) govern everything you do and you should become accustomed to visualizing the impact of data on the web both in terms of what you interact with and how the data you produce "gets out there".

Do not be afraid to try out different formats to see what works best for you. While being guided by the data in terms of content quality is fine, it is also good to be certain of your convictions in terms of what you're projecting. Many times, your most popular content is not the one that reaches the right audience. Popular content helps expand your reach and it should become an aid to finding more of your right audience. It is a fine balancing act that always needs to be informed by your core values and mission. This is an ever-ongoing activity much as it is in real life and as such it should never take place without some thought and consideration.

Semantic Search Action List for Step #18

1. List influencers in your industry that you know, who could be persuaded to help you amplify the content you share and the message of your posts.

2. List influencers in your industry that you know, whose content and posts would make a good fit in your online social media sharing. Reshare their content and acknowledge their work.

3. List all your peers and the ways you could support them with your content.

4. List all the ways you think your peers could support your own or your brand's digital presence.

5. List all the potential brand ambassadors you could enlist to help amplify your social signal.

6. List the values of your brand that align with the values of those in your social network. Your content creation strategy must help them achieve their own identity curation.

7. Put in place an action plan to monitor mentions of your brand and content on social media platforms. Then amplify those comments and responses by resharing them and focus on some of the highlights.

8. Encourage comments and resharing of your content and social media posts by engaging with those who respond to them.

9. Create a structured schedule for all your social media sharing activity. Then create set times when you respond to comments, reshares and further engagement.

10. Create a cross-format content sharing action plan so that your videos and podcasts surface alongside your text-driven content and posts and vice versa.

Step #19 "From strings to things"

 # The semantic web is about being real, developing authority and expertise and establishing your identity.

If you've read each chapter sequentially you have, by now, taken 18 steps each of which is designed to help you create a more granular, very focused and highly visible presence across the web and across mobile devices. A presence that takes full advantage of the artificial intelligence driven core of search.

Each step has been incremental, to some extent, building on what has been covered before and addressing the overlaps in ways designed to help you with your action steps.

You will have, by now, also answered in detail some 180 of these action steps designed to help you establish a methodology that will help your SEO regardless of what upgrades Google makes to its search engine.

There are really only two more steps to read and just twenty more action steps left to take. This chapter then, is your 'breather' before the final sprint. It is the primer intended to give you the context to understand where your efforts go and why everything you have been reading and everything you have been doing, really matters.

The web that used to be a decentralized, anonymous place where anyone could be anything is fast becoming a hierarchical, structured place where value and reputation revolve around authority and identity.

This is part of Google's publicly stated effort to take the web "from strings to things" which means from code to people and places and objects. This is all part of its semantic search indexing.

What this means for you is that many of the technologies that were being used to index and rank a website in search led to effects that could be reverse-engineered and applied to achieve them.

This was regardless of whether a website was worth that kind of attention or not. It also meant that those who could afford to pay more could hire people who knew how to game search and would therefore rise in the search engine results pages (SERPs) regardless of quality.

I admit it was a tad unfair. It also flew against the values of the web which was the great equalizer. The place where a small business with a tiny budget, a lot of passion and great ideas, could take on a much bigger rival and win.

Well, rejoice. That lofty ideal is back. And it is here to stay. Now, don't get me wrong. Truckloads of money and an army of willing social media marketers can still generate some traction. But whereas in the past all this 'noise' was all that was required to help a large company win the marketing game, now all it will do is add to the confusion of its signal. Any gains made will be short-lived which means it will not be too long before the website in question drops out of sight and stays there.

Signal (with a capital S) is really what semantic search and the semantic web and every step in this book is all about. It is about you (either as an individual with something to market or a company with something to sell) finding "you". The real you. The sense of self that allows you to function, that makes those who work for you and with you do so willingly, the part of you which makes you work the way you do and do what you do. All of this is part of your identity. Just like no two people are really alike, no two companies or businesses can ever be alike even if they do the exact same thing.

As people we go through quite a painful process of childhood and adolescence where we struggle with the concept of who we are and what we are meant to do in the world. I find it incredible that entire businesses spring up without ever having undergone that same soul-searching. Now, here's what happens when we, as people, don't. We grow up, get a job (and maybe even start a family), enjoy a career and, at some point in our lives, we kinda 'wake up' and have a mental or psychological breakdown.

It's not that anything has drastically changed around us. It's just that we realized that we barely make an impact on the world, we hardly exist and just existing is far from easy. The realization is enough to make us falter.

Businesses that fail to successfully internalize their identity also have similar breakdowns for very similar reasons.

The fix is easy enough, of course, and the sooner it's applied the more effective it will be: find out who you really are. Where do the proverbial lines you will not cross lie? What do you really want to stand for at the core of your being (even if that being is figurative and your business is huge).

Define all this and you define you. Define you and your path appears clearer. None of this is easy. Actually this is the hardest chapter in the book because the actionables required are time-consuming.

The point is that however long it takes, you simply cannot escape this. It has to be done. The upside is that if you do it, you will never have to worry about 'learning' SEO or getting your marketing 'right'. These things become way easier when they are informed by a real sense of mission, a real sense of identity and a real sense of passion.

With zero technical knowledge and marketing knowhow you may end up doing things in a rough-and-ready sort of way at times and yet find that the connection with your audience is there.

It's no coincidence if you find yourself in that situation. People connecting with people, people connecting with brands they really understand, people doing business with companies they trust, is what business has always been about.

The technical stuff you can fix. Even watching how the 'pros' do it will give you sufficient tips to add some polish. No amount of polish however is going to make an insincere marketing message work or help a company that is lying to itself (first) and its public, succeed.

Semantic Search Action List for Step #19

1. List all of your areas of expertise. Check to see if they are all represented in the content you create and the posts you share on social media platforms.

2. Make sure that any official organizations or websites that list your credentials or achievements also mention your website and business.

3. Use the same standardized photograph of yourself across all social media posts and profiles. Make sure the file name when you upload it is your name. Do the same where your business logo is concerned when creating business profiles (i.e.

LinkedIn, Instagram etc), the file name should be the name of your business.

4. Create a naming framework where the file names you upload are reflective of your business name and a brief description.

5. Check all your Alt Text to make sure there is consistency when it comes to your images. Check details such as business name and descriptions that reflect your brand values.

6. Do a search for your name and see if you can claim the Knowledge Panel that will appear on the right-hand side of Google search. (Note, this depends on the amount of information that's been indexed about you.)

7. If you haven't done so already go to Google Maps, enter your business name and claim the business listing. (Instructions on how to do it are here: http://bit.ly/2T1Gxl7).

8. Check all your Calls To Action (CATs). Do they fit in with your identity, style and values? If not seek to bridge the gap of who you say you are and what you do and the way you do it.

9. Verify all the online accounts you can: YouTube, Twitter, Instagram, Amazon, etc.

10. Interlink every verified online account you can so that from one others can be discovered.

Step #20
Links and Keywords

 # Links are dead, so are keywords but not quite in the way you think.

On the internet nothing ever quite dies. It just morphs into something else, with few exceptions. The reason for this lies in the fact that from a functionality point of view, there is a good reason why something exists on the web in the first place and unless the reason goes away that 'something' is not likely to really go away either.

Links and keywords are no exception to this rule. In the past there used to be a very discernible, direct link between a website's visibility on search, the keywords it had been optimized for and the links that it had acquired which gave it a sense of credibility.

In the offline world you can pay friends to say they like you. You can pretend to have a reputation if you pay people enough to say good things about you for a while. In the same way, online, links and keywords were the means through which the system could be gamed and search could be made to return specific websites for specific search queries provided you could pay enough for it.

With semantic search things are not quite so straightforward. 'Soft' values like trustworthiness, expertise and authority take a lot longer to build and even longer to establish and no quick application of keywords or buying of links is going to help.

Domain expertise, the subject matter your website, business or yourself is known for takes real knowledge to establish; and real work to maintain.

Because there is no viable shortcut semantic search promotes soft skills like honesty, transparency and real values as the only viable alternative to establishing trust and building a reputation. This, naturally leads us to the question do keywords still count, do we still need links?

The short answers to these are "yes" and "yes" but there are provisos. If you were creating content in the past based on keywords that now, is no longer a viable option and its practice is likely to lead to the kind of thin-value content that will get your website penalized. If you were creating links based on quid-pro-quo tactics or, worse, buying them, this now has to stop.

What do you do instead? Well, the content you create has to be search-query based. This may naturally contain keywords relevant to your industry and even jargon but it should not contain either in an unnatural writing pattern. You should have in place a content creation plan and you should really be focusing on that. If you're doing your job right in terms of answering search queries and providing value to your online visitors so that they can find answers to the specific questions they have quickly, then keywords become inevitable.

If you are doing your job right in terms of answering search queries … (OK, I would only be repeating myself here), then some links will become inevitable as websites begin to link to your content and social media shares also count as links (though they are of more transient value).

These are old ways of looking at this however. The transition I mentioned is that links are now reflected by relationships and keywords by attributes related to your digital profiles and business.

This is a new way of looking at things. Every relationship you create as a business or a person in the online world is a link that begins to define your identity. Every item of content you create on your website and share through social network platforms or find and share through your social media profiles, is an attribute ascribed to your online identity. These become the keywords you are known by.

The links which give value to your online presence are hard-won today and come from the websites associated with you and your business and the people who interact and actively engage with what you do. The keywords that spring up are the result of content, comments, hashtags and expressed sentiment.

Yes, of course, the traditional view of a link is still valid but it has been seriously deprecated and the traditional view of a keyword is still at play but nowhere as much as it used to be.

So, this, now leaves us with many more moving parts than ever before and things look likely to get even more complicated.

Artificial intelligence is able to decipher patterns of behavior at a much more nuanced level than the previous algorithms Google employed. This makes *all* of your behavior count. Every step we have detailed here, all the steps mentioned in the previous edition of this book. All the engagement, the graphics, the structured data mark ups, the metadata and online activity, the values and the sense of purpose that informs everything your business does.

Provided you stay the course, continue to add density to the data you place online not only in volume (depth) but also in reach and networking capability (breadth), then in the immortal words of the Corrs "You Gonna Be just Fine" - http://goo.gl/q72231.

Semantic Search Action List for Step #20

1. List all the tools you're using to measure your website's performance. Ascribe a value and a definition to each of the metrics you are tracking. For example: traffic that shows reach. Be as scientific as possible in your approach so that what you measure reflects what you need (i.e. a niche site may need more repeat visitors each month than it needs new visitors).

2. List the keywords that are linked to the subject matter of your website.

3. Expand the keywords you have listed into concepts, queries and questions. For instance, in SEO an interest in "keywords" and "link strategies" are designed to answer the question of "How do I make my website rank higher in search?"

4. Your list of concepts, queries and questions should be your content creation map.

5. Check to see if your website content answers every single basic question your target audience has in as comprehensive a way as possible.

6. Use your online engagement with your audience to mine fresh questions to answer in your content.

7. Track your content and social media posts as an ever-evolving narrative. Use your activities to drive, guide and even lead the online conversation on the subject matter of your business.

8. Don't stand still. Project ahead to a year from now, two years from now. Where do you see yourself/your business to be at? Assume that you succeeded. Now work backwards. Take action from the conviction of your success.

9. Check to see if there is any missing information in the subject matter of your business. Something that is maybe a little less obvious or tougher to write about or communicate. Look to see where your competitors may be lacking. Then fill that gap.

10. Review the steps in this book regularly. In SEO, as in business and life, there is no "getting there". Everything is a journey with fluid targets, skillsets and aspirations. Create your own living map out of all this and use it to evolve your business.

Most Frequently Asked Semantic Search Questions

The following SEO questions seem to crop up again and again, in one form or another, in the many emails I receive through my website.

Whenever I can I still answer emails personally putting in as much time and thought as each requires to answer it fully. Beyond the obvious fact that this is my one small contribution to the good karma of the universe it is also a great way to see what issues crop up again and again as busy webmasters struggle with the online marketing and optimization of their websites.

#01. Will Google Ads Help My SEO?

Because Google is in the process of socializing Google Ads, including information about Click Through Rates (CTR) in Google Analytics and integrating the Google +1 Button in display ads, there is now a strong supposition by many webmasters that having Google Ads on their site will help their SEO and their site will be promoted higher in search engines. Actually this is wrong and if anything it is likely to hurt your site by triggering Google's alerts for spam sites or sites with low quality content or sites with poor end-user experience.

#02. Are Underscores Are the Same as Dashes in a Website's URL?

This comes from mostly new webmasters who believe that because usability best practice dictates that a dash is clearer to understand in a URL than an underscore which may get hidden by an underline, then the two are pretty much the same with the exception of dashes being more legible. The truth is that for purely technical reasons which have to do with its origin, Google sees dashes as marks separating words but ignores underscores so, for example Help-My-SEO in a URL would get indexed by Google as three separate words but Help_My_SEO would get indexed as a single word: HelpMySEO. Dashes and underscores are not separate, but they are different and how you use them on your website really depends upon the kind of indexing in terms of search terms, you want to achieve.

#03. Is The Length of Registration of a Website is a Ranking Factor?

Now, this one is a little bit of a bugbear to tackle because there is a sound logic to it and there has been some propagation of the idea through many webmaster forums. It is an unfortunate effect of SEO knowledge that the wrong kind of it is often repeated the most and it is that which get to be believed, for that very reason. The truth is that while some sites which assess the value of a website's SEO status through their own algorithm, do check for the length of time it has been registered for, and then allocate a higher value if it is registered from more than a year, Google does not. Google's algorithm has been fine-tuned to check a website for value, relevancy and original content and it uses well over 200 metrics to do so. The length of time a website is registered for is not one of them.

#04. Does: The Type of Domain you Have Affect your Country-based Indexing?

Google is big on localization and it is one of the main SEO drives since 2012. Its algorithm is sensitive enough to actually check a website's IP address (i.e. its server location) and use that to determine whether it should be in the .com or .com.au or .fr or.de and so on, Google index. This means that you could get a top-level-domain (typically a .com) but if your server is based in France then your site will also get indexed in Google.fr and it will show up there. Google does not leave its filtering at that. It takes into account the Click Through Rates (CTRs) and typical end-user behavior and further adjusts the country-specific indexing and ranking of a website.

#05. Do New Pages Take a Long Time to Get Indexed?

This is another one of those forum-propagated false pieces of information which is treated as gospel by new webmasters. Google can index a brand-new site within minutes of it going live, provided it is linked to by an authority website Google crawls regularly. So, the trick is to make sure that the content of your website is socialized through the major social networks and that will lead the Google bot straight to you.

#06. Where do you use the schema.org tags for a business address?

Do you use them in the contact us page of your website or do you implement it in the home page of the website so that your location shows up when someone searches by the brand name?

This is the correct approach for using Schema with addresses on websites:-

```
<div itemscope=""
itemtype="http://schema.org/ContactPoint">

<div itemscope=""
itemtype="schema.org/PostalAddress">

<span itemprop="name">Clubnet Search
Marketing</span><br>

<span itemprop="streetAddress">Tamar Science Park,
1 Davy Road</span><br>

<span
itemprop="addressLocality">Plymouth</span><br>

<span itemprop="addressRegion">Devon</span><br>

<span itemprop="postalCode">PL6 8BX</span><br>

<span itemprop="addressCountry">United
Kingdom</span><br>

</div>
```

```
<span itemprop="telephone">Tel: <a
href="tel:08452996005">+44 (0)845 299
6005</a></span>

<span itemprop="faxNumber"></span>

</div>
```

You can see the validated markup here: http://goo.gl/AhPN

#07. My website is all about providing links to legitimate companies and makes the html to content ratio pretty high. Should I continue to mark these links as no follow?

Code to content ratios are one single signal, and one that we don't know if the search engines even consider very much. A Panda or Penguin analysis likely looks at a range of signals rather than any single one, so if it makes sense to have that many links in terms of delivering value, by all means, do it. Adding a no-follow to them is only a precaution against automatically triggering Google's low-quality filters.

#08. How do I use Keyword Domains and "Brand Links" now? If brand links are the thing to do now and keyword domains also got devalued, how do you build links for keyword domains?

Exact keyword domains or Exact Match Domains (EMD) are useful if the content on them is good. On its own, an exact keyword domain will not help you anymore. So EMD plus good content plus branded links works well.

But if anything in that equation delivers less than top quality then you may be in trouble.

#09. How important is duplicate content when you cannot avoid it?

It is true that Google frowns against duplicate content. Although it is not an instant demotion in terms of ranking in search it is a fairly strong signal that can be amplified when it is combined with other signals that may indicate that your website is not as good as you think it to be. Bottom line, duplicate content is an easy fix. Other signals may not be. So you ought to address it. There is a caveat here that in those cases where duplicate content may be unavoidable or you can do nothing about it, just let it go. Concentrate on each page you create to be as strong as possible in terms of the information it contains and the value it provides.

#10. Does Google put a lot of store by authorship in articles and posts?

It really depends on what you mean by "a lot of store". In keeping with its intent to establish real-world knowledge Google looks to create as comprehensive an author graph as possible. Establishing clear ownership of the content you write and the posts you share is good practice. It also helps Google (and other search engines) determine your level of authority on specific subjects and even your trustworthiness.

#11. Is Facebook's Graph Search still active?

No. Graph search as a natural language semi-structured search engine is gone. It's been replaced by a more keyword-based search engine focused on posts.

However if you make queries similar to the ones graph search used to answer, such as "Friends who live in Sacramento" then there will be a section of results pointing you to that structured query. So, parts of Graph Search are active but hidden within Facebook's current search function.

#12. I heard the Google's First Page does not exist anymore. I see it all the time so what does that mean?

Google's "First Page" made perfect sense when all there was to worry about was desktop search. Now we have extensive fragmentation of search into Voice Search, Google Assistant, google Maps, YouTube, Waze, Google Mobile Search. Each of these uses the data it has about you, your search preferences and your social history to customize the results you see on Google search. So although there still is a "First Page" it is a little bit different for every user depending on a large variety of factors. This is why using just the ranking of certain pages of your site as a measure of success in you SEO is no longer enough. The best measure is increased traffic as it means you are getting increased visibility and increased relevant traffic as it means your business and website are appearing as an answer to search queries specific to your business.

#13. Does a WordPress blog give you any SEO advantage with Google?

Yes and no. There is no easy "SEO advantage" you can get with anything. The WordPress organization however has worked closely with Google to create a platform that is somewhat easier to index and perhaps easier to optimize than many of its rivals. Having said that I have seen plenty of examples of WordPress blogs that were simply so bad at SEO that they failed to rank for what they were promoting.

#14. Is semantic search all about structured data?

At face value, yes. The web however is full of unstructured data that is being crawled and indexed in a structured way. This means that implementing structured data on your website is not going to give you any natural SEO advantage over a website that hasn't got structured data. It will however help Google search understand what your website is about more easily. That's a major first hurdle. Content quality and the end-user experience however are still key to having success with a website in search.

#15. Is there a simple change I can make to my website that would instantly help its SEO?

As it happens this impossible question has a real answer. If you get your website hosted on a real cloud server, the increased uptime, stability and speed gains made will give you a slight SEO edge. Notice, I only said slight, but it will be an instant improvement even though you will not have done any other SEO work on your website.

#16. My pictures suck. What if I use pictures I find on the web to illustrate my website?

Well, there is a little thing called copyright that might cause a few problems there. Plus you may find it difficult to rank on Google's Image Search for images that already exist elsewhere. I would suggest you take your own photographs or find images at one of the many royalty free image sites across the web and try to make them as unique to you as possible.

#17. Is link building still important now?

Link building is not dead as an SEO activity by any means. It is however a lot more selective. The key now is quality. The backlinks you create to your website simply have to be impeccable. The understanding of a link's value in the semantic web has changed a little. See Step #20 for more details.

#18. Are keywords useless in the new SEO world?

No. keywords are still in play. In fact everything we have learnt about SEO over the last 18 years still holds true. But each element gets more and more deprecated and it then becomes part of a very complex search ranking equation that requires the right combination of elements in the right proportion to come together, so a website can rank. Keywords now work as a linked function of content attributes and domain authority (i.e. your expertise as a business entity or person) – see Step #20 for more details.

#19. I am planning to guest blog a lot this year to help promote my website. Is this a valid SEO technique?

Guest blogging can still be useful. It provides you with a link to your website, gives you a new platform to work from which means you stand a good chance of finding a fresh audience and it can provide you with a citation boost in Google's eyes. Guest blogging takes time and effort and energy so be picky with the blogs you choose to write for. Make sure they are relevant, respected and within the subject matters your business generally covers. Google has gone to great lengths to close the loopholes associated with guest blogging so the bottom line is that if you would not choose to be associated with a website if they did not give you a link, you should not blog for them just to get a link.

#20. My website was hit hard in the last Google update. I lost 75% of my traffic and ranking. Is it worth trying to fix it or should I scrap it and start with a fresh domain?

This is probably the hardest question to answer accurately. Google updates are not penalties. They are algorithmic changes to Google's search ranking. This means a website can recover if the issues it got hit for are fixed (namely, low quality content and links coming from suspect websites). In practice this may not always be possible. It really comes down to how much good content you have on your website and how closely is it tied up to your branding. If it is part and parcel of everything else you do then you have no choice, fix the content and focus on being the best online business you can possibly be .

Remember that success in search is a marathon not a sprint. Nothing happens overnight and everything has to be part of a coherent, logical whole.

Famous Last Words

This is the page where I leave you with some thoughts and perhaps explain anything which needs further clarification.

SEO is not dead and it is not going to go away. As the web becomes more complex and semantic search begins to fully grip we will get to see less and less of its inner workings and it will become more and more nuanced and harder to game.

This is a cycle of development that we have already seen with the PC and those of you who struggled with the infernal Windows 95 will understand what is meant by the "Blue Screen of Death" which has become a rarity in our days.

SEO is like that. Google has already stopped announcing when they make changes to their search algorithm creating a sense of insecurity in an already paranoid SEO community. The plus side of this is that you should now focus on doing what your business does best:

delivering value to its online customers. That should be the overriding concern you should have and everything you do should be seen through this perspective.

The 20 steps you have just finished reading work. They are far from exhaustive as far as SEO goes but then again they were never designed to be a complete guide to it. What you want is to get your website to enjoy an increased presence in search across devices. Increased ranking and increased traffic. This will most definitely happen as long as you continue to work along the lines suggested by these 20 steps.

I have worked hard to make the instructions throughout this book as simple as possible so I have nothing to add that needs to be explained further, here.

SEO, for me, represents an opportunity. The chance to prove that armed with a little knowledge, a website, a good business plan and passion, a small business can create as good an experience and presence on the web as a big one, and do it better.

I really believe this. The semantic web, again, is the great equalizer. Work on your SEO. Focus on your success. Prove me right. Win big.

Talk to me

If you Google me you will find out pretty much everything you need to know about me. For the record I am a journalist who passed, for a while, as a business exec in a suit. I am very active on LinkedIn (please feel free to join me there) and you can follow me on Twitter: @davidamerland. I blog a lot about social media, business development and SEO, some of it is on my own website: www.davidamerland.com. If this book has helped you please tell all your friends about it. If you think it can be improved in any way, please tell me.

Other books by the author

The Sniper Mind: Eliminate Fear, Deal with Uncertainty, and Make Better Decisions

Google Semantic Search: Search Engine Optimization (SEO) Techniques That Gets Your Company More Traffic, Increases Brand Impact and Amplifies Your Online Presence

The Social Media Mind: How Social Media is Changing Business, Politics and Science and Helps Create a New World Order

Brilliant Search Engine Optimisation (SEO)

Getting to No. 1 on Google in Simple Steps

Online Marketing Help: How to Promote Your Online Business Using Twitter, Facebook, MySpace and Other Social Networks

SEO Help: 20 search engine optimization steps to get your website to Google's #1 page

Bibliography

1. Moldovan, D.I., Mihalcea, R.: Using wordnet and lexical operators to improve internet searches. IEEE Internet Computing 4 (2000) 34–43

2. Buscaldi, D., Rosso, P., Arnal, E.S.: A wordnet-based query expansion method for geographical information retrieval. In: Working Notes for the CLEF Workshop. (2005)

3. Kruse, P.M., Naujoks, A., Roesner, D., Kunze, M.: Clever search: A wordnet based wrapper for internet search engines. In: Proceedings of the 2nd GermaNet Workshop. (2005)

4. Guha, R., McCool, R., Miller, E.: Semantic search. In: WWW '03: Proceedings of the 12th international conference on World Wide Web, ACM Press (2003) 700–709

5. Rocha, C., Schwabe, D., de Aragao, M.P.: A hybrid approach for searching in the semantic web. In: Proceedings of the 13th international conference on World Wide Web. (2004) 374–3836. Airio, E., Jarvelin, K., Saatsi, P., Kek ¨ al¨ ainen, J., Suomela, S.: Ciri - an ontology-based query interface for text retrieval. In Hyvonen, E., Kauppinen, T., Salminen, M., Viljanen, K., Ala-Siuru, P., eds.: Web Intelligence: Proceedings of the 11th Finnish Artificial Intelligence Conference. (2004)

7. Heflin, J., Hendler, J.: Searching the web with shoe (2000)

8. Maedche, A., Staab, S., Stojanovic, N., Studer, R., Sure, Y.: Seal - a framework for developing semantic web portals. In: Advances in Databases, Proceedings of the 18th British National Conference on Databases. (2001) 1–22

9. Makel ¨ a, E., Hyv ¨ onen, E., Sidoroff, T.: View-based user interfaces for information retrieval on the semantic web. In: Proceedings of the ISWC-2005 Workshop End User Semantic Web Interaction. (2005)

10. Makel ¨ a, E., Hyv ¨ onen, E., Saarela, S., Viljanen, K.: OntoViews - A Tool for Creating Semantic Web Portals. In: Proceedings of the Third Internation Semantic Web Conference, Springer Verlag (2004)

11. Reynolds, D., Shabajee, P., Cayzer, S.: Semantic Information Portals. In: Proceedings of the 13th International World Wide Web Conference on Alternate track papers & posters, ACM Press (2004)

12. Hyvonen, E., M ¨ akel ¨ a, E., Salminen, M., Valo, A., Viljanen, K., Saarela, S., Junnila, M., Kettula, S. Museumfinland – finnish museums on the semantic web. Web Semantics: Science, Services and Agents on the World Wide Web 3 (2005) 224–241

13. Hyvonen, E., M ¨ akel ¨ a, E.: Semantic autocompletion. (2005)

14. Makel ¨ a, E., Viljanen, K., Lindgren, P., Laukkanen, M., Hyv ¨ onen, E.: Semantic yellow page service discovery: The veturi portal. In: Poster paper, 4th International Semantic Web Conference. (2005)

15. Karger, D.R., Bakshi, K., Huynh, D., Quan, D., Sinha, V.: Haystack: A general-purpose information management tool for end users based on semistructured data. In: Proceedings of the CIDR Conference. (2005) 13–26

16. Quan, D., Huynh, D., Karger, D.R.: Haystack: A platform for authoring end user semantic web applications. In: Proceedings of the Second International Semantic Web Conference. (2003) 738–753

17. Teevan, J., Alvarado, C., Ackerman, M.S., Karger, D.R.: The perfect search engine is not enough: a study of orienteering behavior in directed search. In: Proceedings of the Conference on Human Factors in Computing Systems, CHI. (2004) 415–422

18. Athanasis, N., Christophides, V., Kotzinos, D.: Generating on the fly queries for the semantic web: The ics-forth graphical rql interface (grql). In: Proceedings of the Third International Semantic Web Conference. (2004) 486–501

19. Catarci, T., Dongilli, P., Mascio, T.D., Franconi, E., Santucci, G., Tessaris, S.: An ontology based visual tool for query formulation support. In: Proceedings of the 16th Eureopean Conference on Artificial Intelligence, IOS Press (2004) 308–312.

20. Kaufmann, E.: Talking to the Semantic Web — Natural Language Query Interfaces for Casual End-Users. PhD thesis, University of Zurich (2007)

21. Balog, K., Serdyukov, P., de Vries, A.P.: Overview of the TREC 2011 Entity Track. In: TREC 2011 Working Notes

22. Halpin, H., Herzig, D.M., Mika, P., Blanco, R., Pound, J., Thompson, H.S., Tran, D.T.: Evaluating Ad-Hoc Object Retrieval. In: Proc. IWEST 2010 Workshop

23. Cleverdon, C.W.: Report on the first stage of an investigation onto the comparative efficiency of indexing systems. Technical report, The College of Aeronautics, Cranfield, England (1960) 3512 Elbedweihy, Wrigley, Ciravegna, Reinhard and Bernstein

24. Tummarello, G., Oren, E., Delbru, R.: Sindice.com: Weaving the Open Linked Data. In: Proc. ISWC/ASWC 2007

25. d'Aquin, M., Baldassarre, C., Gridinoc, L., Angeletou, S., Sabou, M., Motta, E. Characterizing Knowledge on the Semantic Web with Watson. In: EON. (2007) 1–10

26. Lopez, V., Motta, E., Uren, V.: PowerAqua: Fishing the Semantic Web. In: The Semantic Web: Research and Applications. (2006) 393–410

27. Damljanovic, D., Agatonovic, M., Cunningham, H.: Natural Language Interface to Ontologies: combining syntactic analysis and ontology-based lookup through the user interaction. In: Proc. ESWC. (2010)

28. Mika, P. (2007) Ontologies are us: A unified model of social networks and semantics. Journal of Web Semantics 5(1), 5–15.

29. Moorman, C., Deshpande, R. and Zaltman, G. (1993) "Factors Affecting Trust in Market Research Relationships," Journal of Marketing, 57 (January), 81-101

30. Mui, L., Halberstadt, A. and Mohtashemi, M. (2002) "Notions of Reputation in Multi-Agents Systems: A Review", Proc. of 1st Int. Joint Conference on Autonomous Agents and Multi-agent Systems (AAMAS 2002), Bologna, Italy, 2002.

31. Noble, C.H., Noble, S.M. and Adjei, M.T. (2012) "Let them talk! Managing primary and extended online brand communities for success", Business Horizons, Vol. 55, Iss. 5, 475–483.

32. Tserpes, K., Papadakis, G., Kardara, M., Papaoikonomou, A., Aisopos, F., Sardis E. and Varvarigou. T. (2012) "SocIoS: A Social Media Application Ontology", On the Move to Meaningful Internet Systems: OTM 2012 Workshops. Lecture Notes in Computer Science Vol. 7567, pp. 574-584. Viljanen, L. (2005) "Towards an ontology of trust", Proc. of the 2nd int. conf. on Trust, Privacy, and Security in Digital Business (TrustBus'05), Springer-Verlag, Berlin, Heidelberg, 175-184.

33. R. Arandjelovic and A. Zisserman. Multiple queries for large scale specific object retrieval. In BMVC, 2012.

34. F. Basura and T. Tuytelaars. Mining multiple queriesfor image retrieval: On-the-fly learning of an object-specific mid-level representation. In ICCV, 2013.

35. G. G. Duffy. Explaining Reading, Second Edition: A Resource for Teaching Concepts, Skills, and Strategies. Guilford Press, 2009.

36. T. Mikolov, W.-t. Yih, and G. Zweig. Linguistic regularities in continuous space word representations. In Proceedings of NAACL-HLT, 2013.

37. J. Pujara, H. Miao, L. Getoor, and W. Cohen. Knowledge Graph Identification. In Proceedings of the 12th International Semantic Web Conference - Part I, ISWC '13, pages 542–557, New York, USA, 2013. Springer.

38. A. Singhal. Introducing the Knowledge Graph: Things, not Strings, May 2012. https://googleblog.blogspot.co. at/2012/05/introducing-knowledge-graph-things-not. html [August, 2019].

39. T. Steiner, R. Verborgh, R. Troncy, J. Gabarr´o Vall´es, and R. Van de Walle. Adding Realtime Coverage to the Google Knowledge Graph. In Poster and Demo Proceedings of the 11th International Semantic Web Conference, Nov. 2012.

40. F. M. Suchanek and G. Weikum. Knowledge Bases in the Age of Big Data Analytics. Proceedings of the VLDB Endowment, 7(13):1713–1714, Aug. 2014.

41. A. Tonon, M. Catasta, R. Prokofyev, G. Demartini, K. Aberer, and P. Cudr´e-Mauroux. Contextualized Ranking of Entity Types Based on Knowledge Graphs. Journal of Web Semantics: Science, Services and Agents on the

World Wide Web, Special Issue on Knowledge Graphs(C):170–183, Mar. 2016.

42. R. Akerkar and P. Sajja. Knowledge-Based Systems. Jones and Bartlett Publishers, USA, 1st edition, 2009.

43. R. Blanco, B. B. Cambazoglu, P. Mika, and N. Torzec. Entity Recommendations in Web Search. In Proceedings of the 12th International Semantic Web Conference - Part II, ISWC '13, pages 33–48, New York, USA, 2013. Springer.

Page deliberately left blank

Page deliberately left blank

Page deliberately left blank

www.ingramcontent.com/pod-product-compliance
Ingram Content Group UK Ltd.
Pitfield, Milton Keynes, MK11 3LW, UK
UKHW021051270726
13967UKWH00012B/570

9 781844 810307